A-Z YORK

CONTENTS

REFERENCE

A Road	A64	City Wall (large scale only)		ꖴꖴꖴꖴ
B Road	B1224	Cycleway (selected)		🚲
Dual Carriageway		Fire Station		■
One-way Street	→	Hospital		Ⓗ
Traffic flow on A Roads is also indicated by a heavy line on the driver's left.	→	House Numbers (A & B Roads only)		13 / 8
Restricted Access		Information Centre		🅸
Pedestrianized Road		National Grid Reference		445
Track / Footpath	====-----	Park & Ride		Grimston Bar P+🚌
Residential Walkway	············	Police Station		▲
Railway	Station / Tunnel / Level Crossing	Post Office		★
Built-up Area	UNION ST	River Boat Trip (large scale only)		🚢
Local Authority Boundary		Toilet:		
Posttown Boundary		without facilities for the Disabled		▽
Postcode Boundary (within Posttown)		with facilities for the Disabled		▽
Map Continuation	16 / Large Scale City Centre 2	Educational Establishment		◩
		Hospital or Hospice		◩
		Industrial Building		◩
		Leisure or Recreational Facility		◩
Car Park (selected)	P	Place of Interest		◩
		Public Building		◩
Church or Chapel	†	Shopping Centre or Market		◩
		Other Selected Buildings		◩

SCALE

Map Pages 4-59 1:15,840	Map Pages 2-3 1:7,920
0 — ¼ — ½ Mile	0 — ⅛ — ¼ Mile
0 — 250 — 500 — 750 Metres	0 — 100 — 200 — 300 Metres
4 inches (10.16 cm) to 1 mile 6.31 cm to 1 kilometre	8 inches (20.32 cm) to 1 mile 12.63 cm to 1 kilometre

Copyright of Geographers' A-Z Map Company Limited

Fairfield Road, Borough Green, Sevenoaks, Kent TN15 8PP
Telephone: 01732 781000 (Enquiries & Trade Sales)
01732 783422 (Retail Sales)
www.a-zmaps.co.uk

Copyright © Geographers' A-Z Map Co. Ltd.

Ordnance Survey® This product includes mapping data licensed from Ordnance Survey® with the permission of the Controller of Her Majesty's Stationery Office.

© Crown Copyright 2007. All rights reserved. Licence number 100017302

Edition 1 2008

C000246699

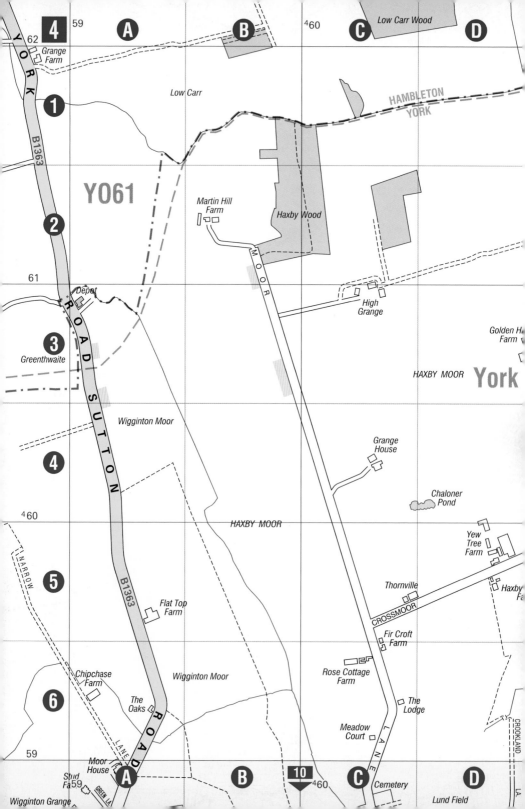

4 59 **A** **B** ⁴60 **C** Low Carr Wood **D**

62

YORK

Grange Farm

1 Low Carr

HAMBLETON
YORK

B1363

YO61

Martin Hill Farm

2 Haxby Wood

MOOR

61

Depot

3

Greenthwaite

High Grange

HAXBY MOOR **York**

ROAD SUTTON

Wigginton Moor

Grange House

4

Golden H Farm

Chaloner Pond

⁴60

HAXBY MOOR

Yew Tree Farm

5

B1363

Thornville Haxby Fa

CROSSMOOR

Flat Top Farm

Fir Croft Farm

NARROW

Chipchase Farm

Rose Cottage Farm

6

The Oaks

Wigginton Moor

The Lodge

ROAD

LANE

Meadow Court

CROOKLAND LA

59

Moor House

Stud Fa 59

GREEN LA

LANE

A **B** **10** ⁴60 **C** Cemetery **D**

Wigginton Grange Lund Field

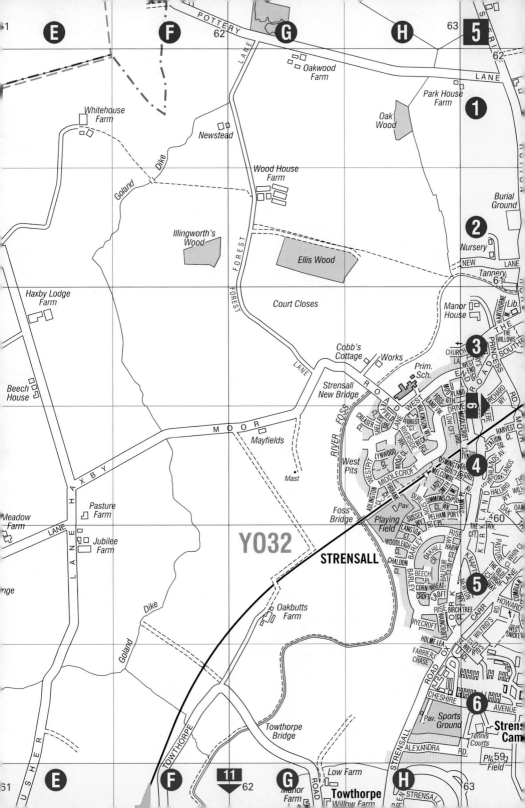

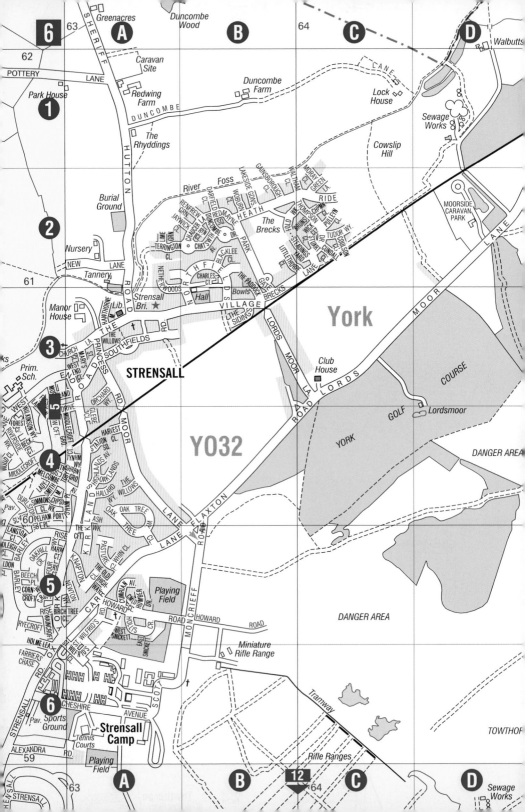

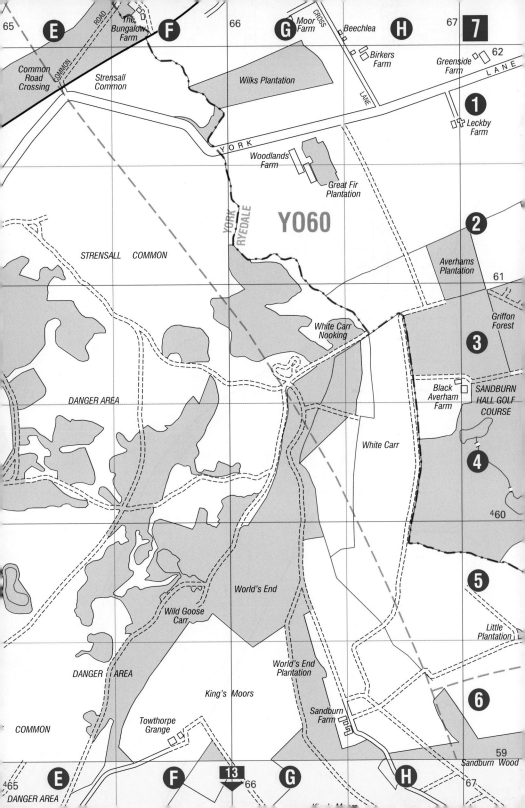

E **F** Moor
Farm **G** Beechlea **H** 67 **7**

The
Bungalow
Farm

Birkers
Farm

Common
Road
Crossing

Strensall
Common

Greenside
Farm 62

LANE

Wilks Plantation

LANE

1

YORK

Leckby
Farm

Woodlands
Farm

Great Fir
Plantation

2

STRENSALL COMMON

YORK RYEDALE

YO60

Averhams
Plantation

61

Griffon
Forest

White Carr
Nooking

3

DANGER AREA

Black
Averham
Farm

SANDBURN
HALL GOLF
COURSE

White Carr

4

⁴60

5

World's End

Little
Plantation

Wild Goose
Carr

DANGER AREA

World's End
Plantation

6

King's Moors

COMMON

Towthorpe
Grange

Sandburn
Farm

59
Sandburn Wood

DANGER AREA

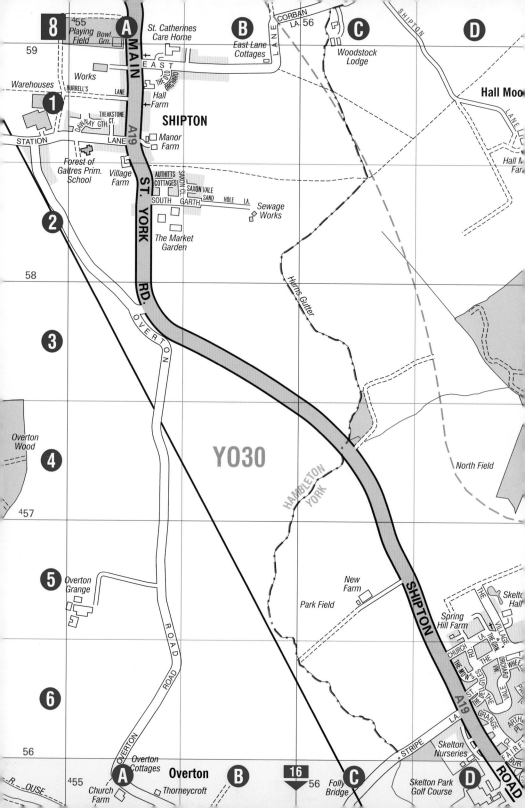

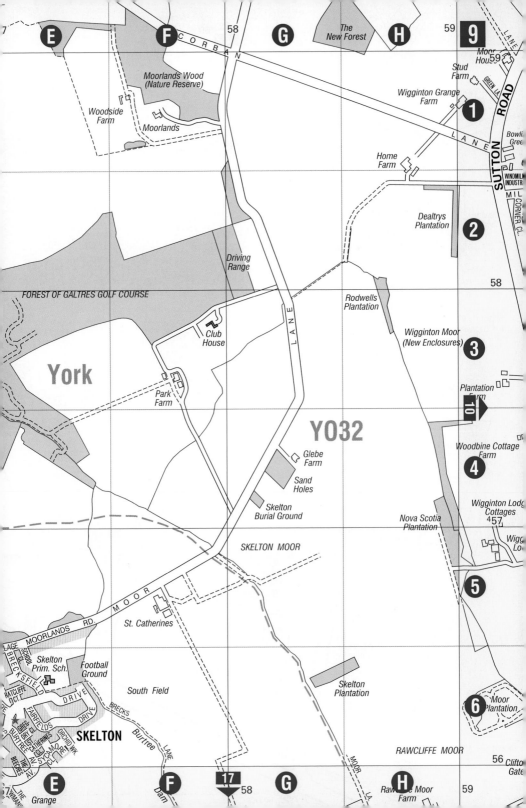

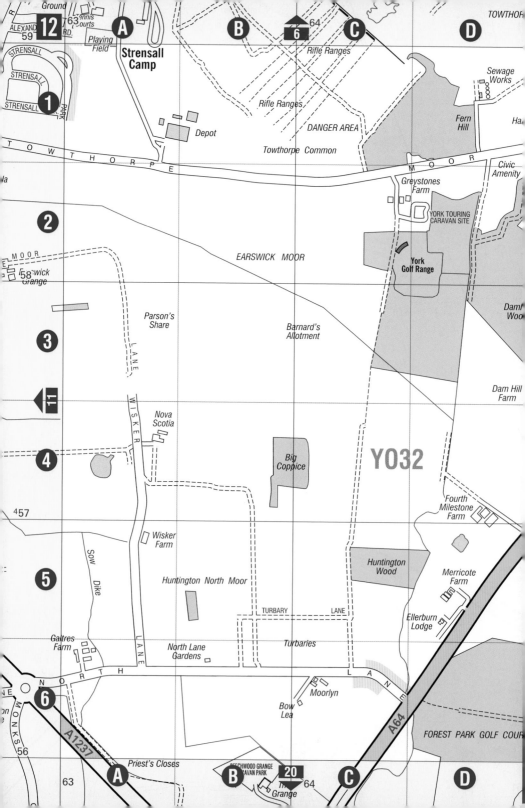

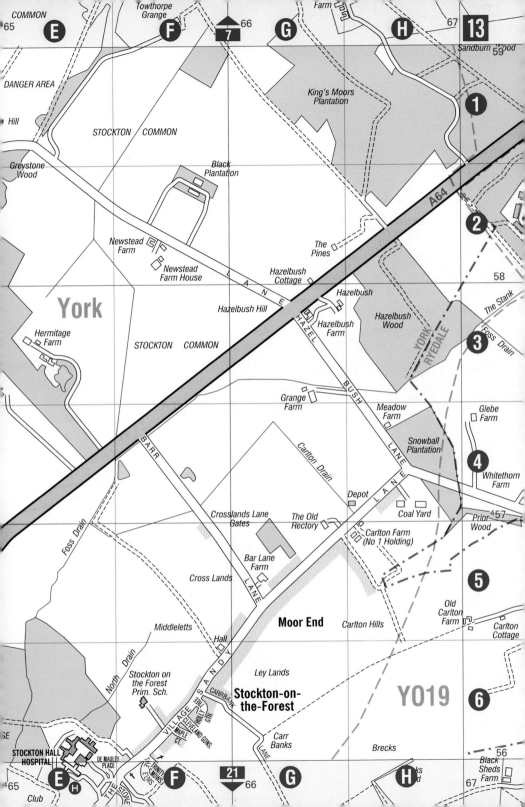

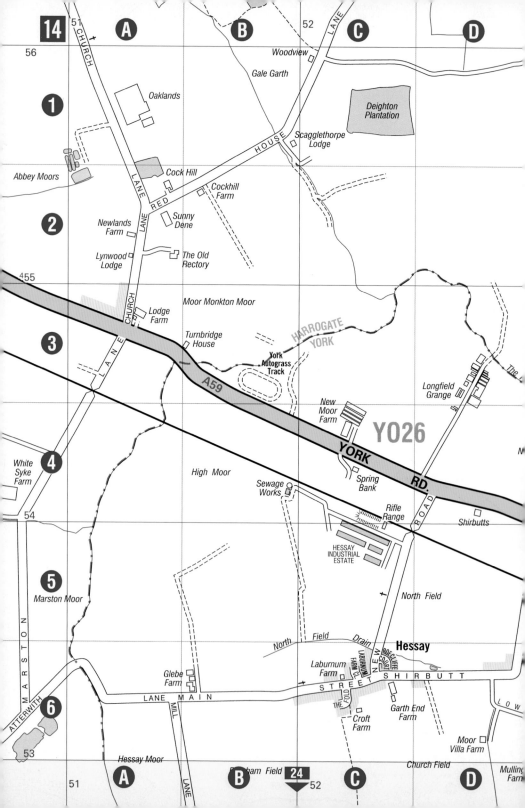

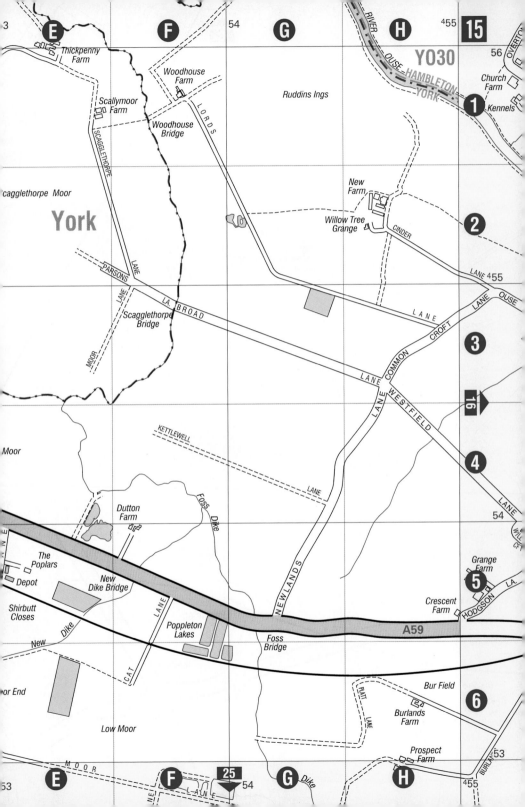

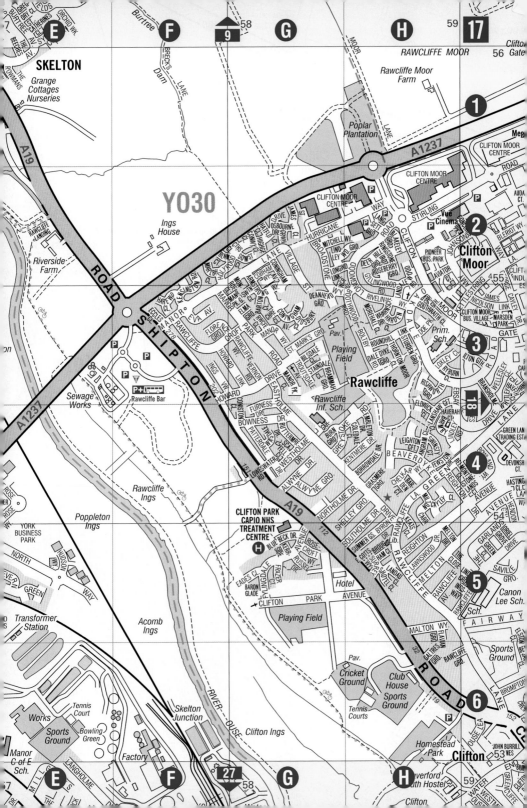

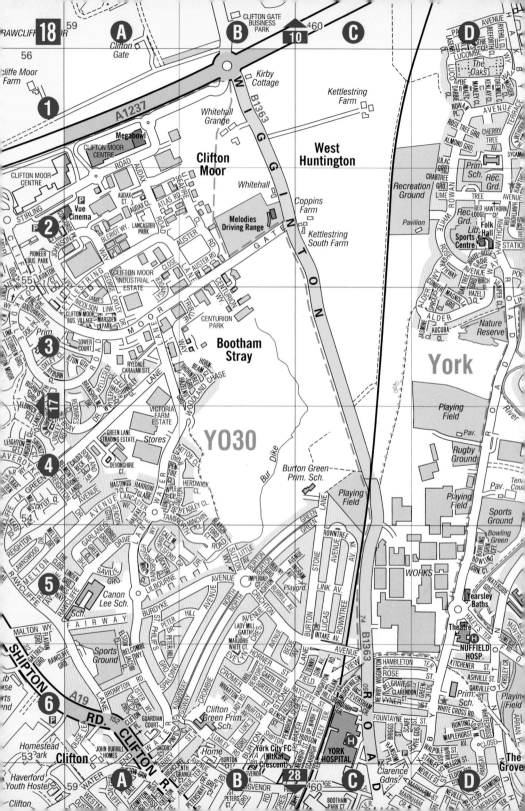

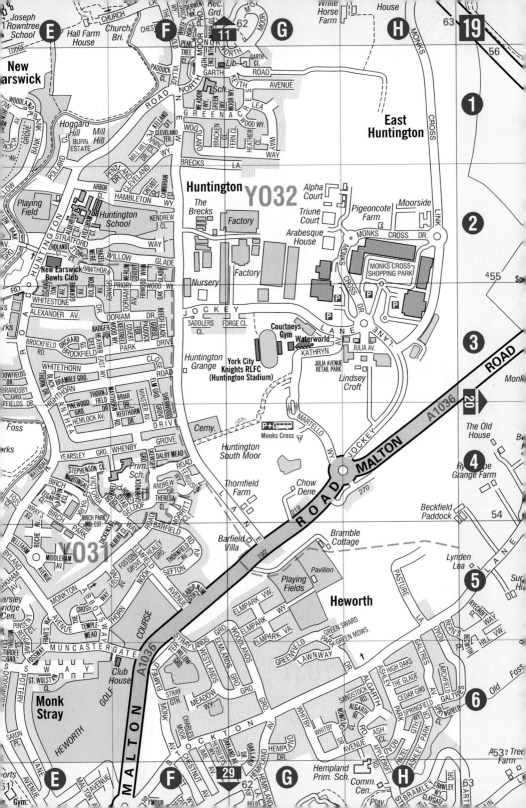

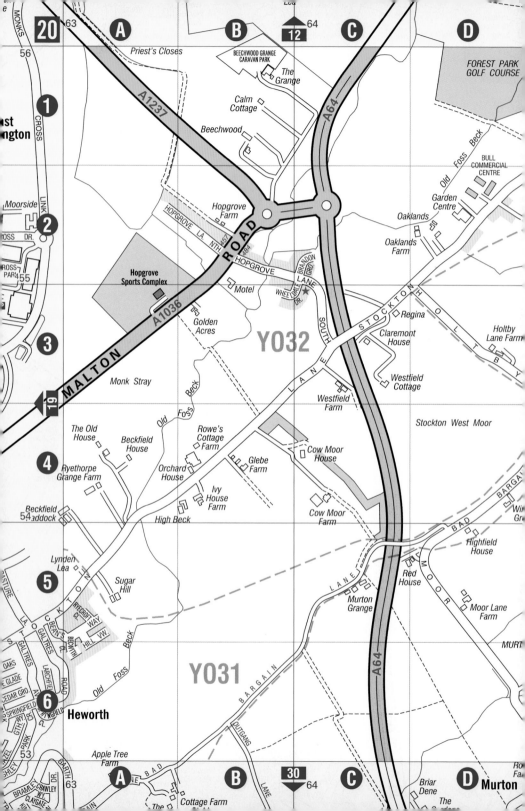

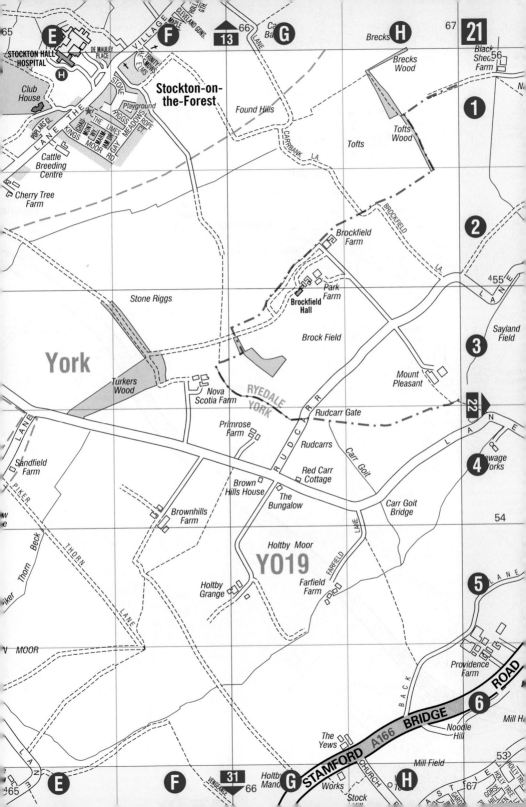

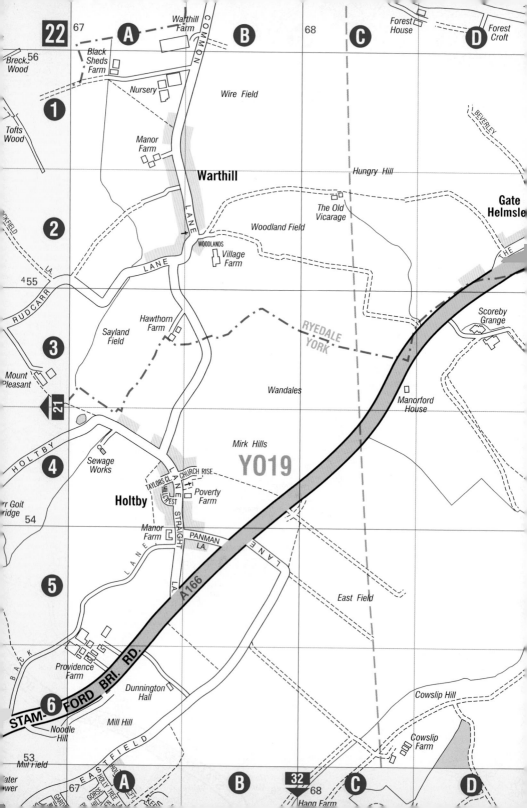

22 67

A
Warthill Farm

B
68

C
Forest House

D
Forest Croft

Breck Wood 56
Black Sheds Farm
Nursery
Wire Field

1

Tofts Wood

Manor Farm

Warthill

Hungry Hill

Gate Helmsle

BEVERLEY

The Old Vicarage
Woodland Field

2
55
RUDCARR LA.
LANE
LANE
COMMON LANE
WOODLANDS
Village Farm

THE

Scoreby Grange

RYEDALE
YORK

Hawthorn Farm

3
Sayland Field

Mount Pleasant

21

Wandales

Manorford House

Mirk Hills
YO19

HOLTBY

Sewage Works

4

r Goit ridge 54

TAYLORS CL.
CHURCH RISE
HILLCREST
LANE
Poverty Farm

Holtby

Manor Farm

STRAIGHT LANE
PANMAN LA.

5
A166

East Field

6
STAM- FORD BRI. RD.
Providence Farm
Dunnington Hall
BACK

Noodle Hill
Mill Hill

53
Mill Field
ater wer

EASTFIELD
GORSE HILL
HOLLY TREE LA.

A
67

B

C
32
68

D

Cowslip Hill

Cowslip Farm

Hagg Farm

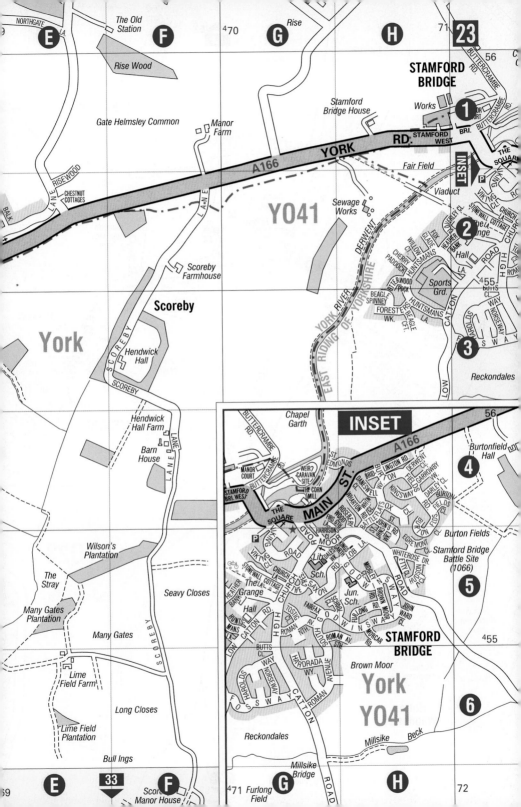

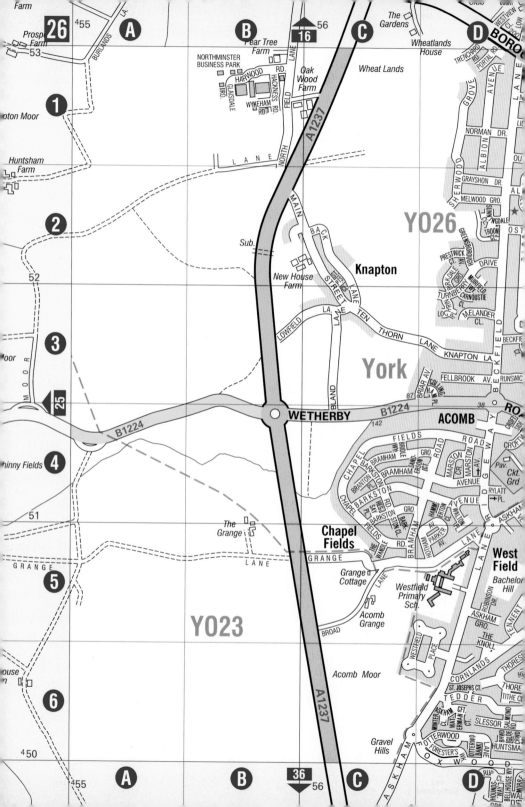

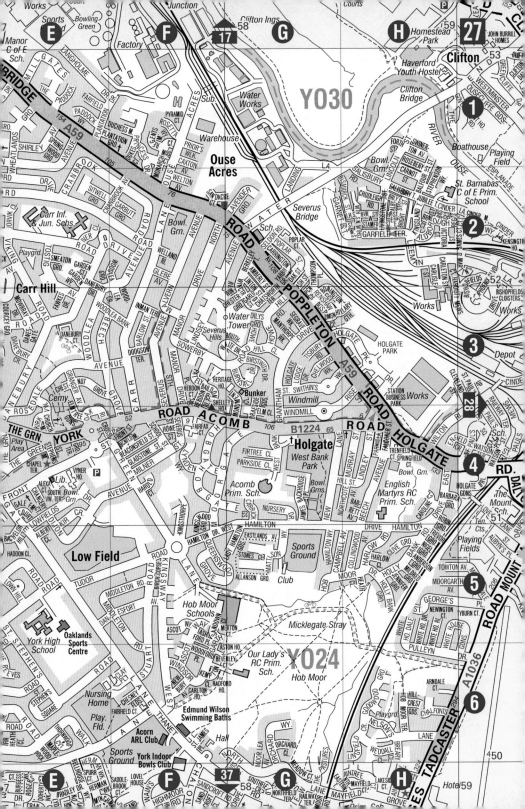

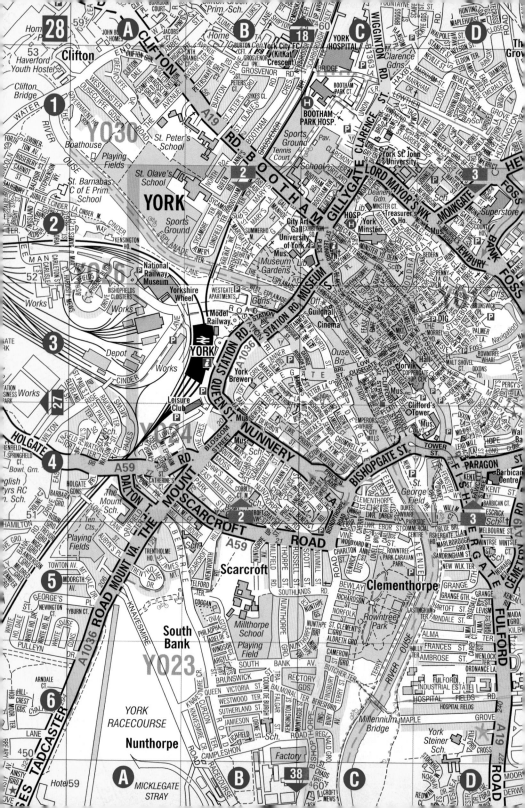

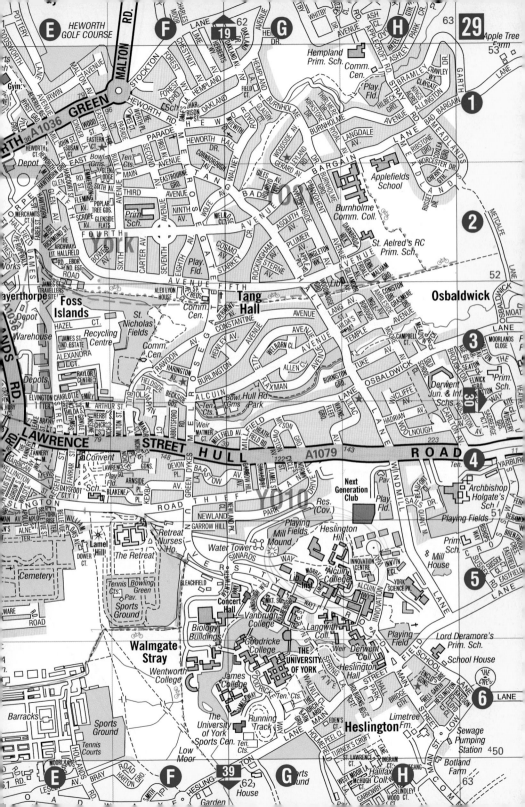

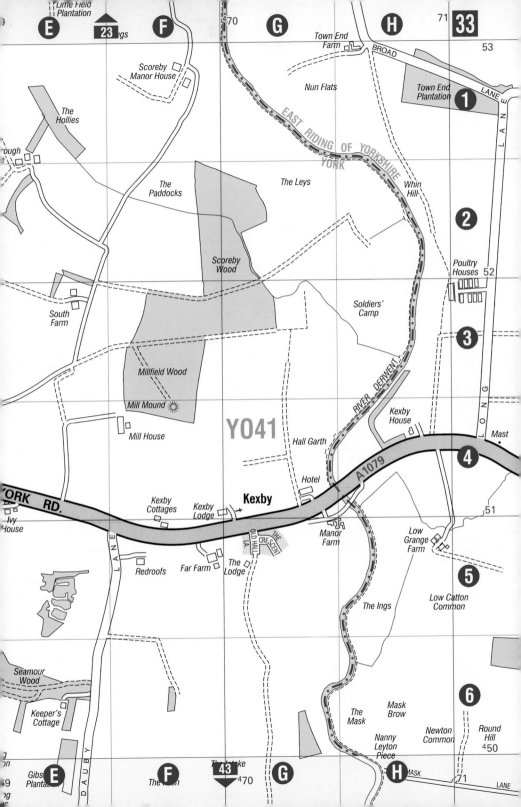

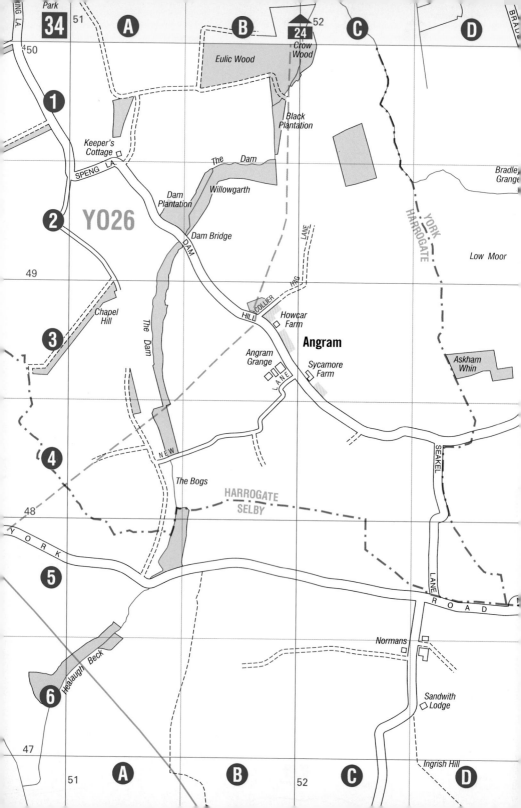

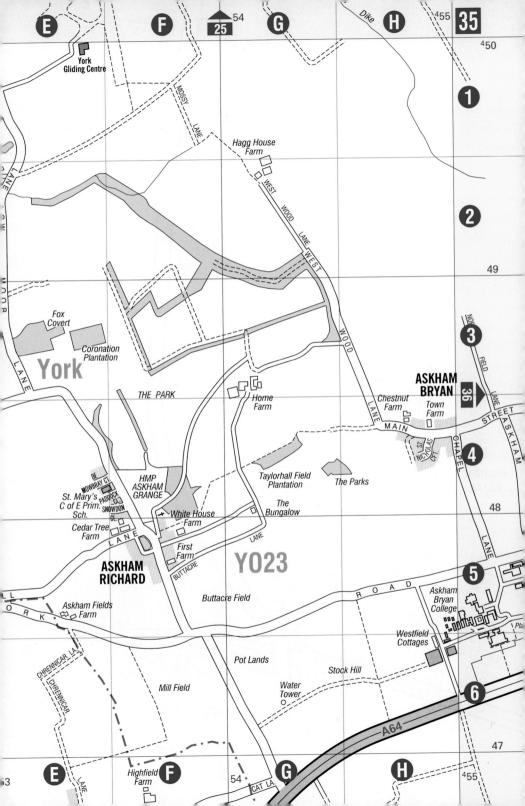

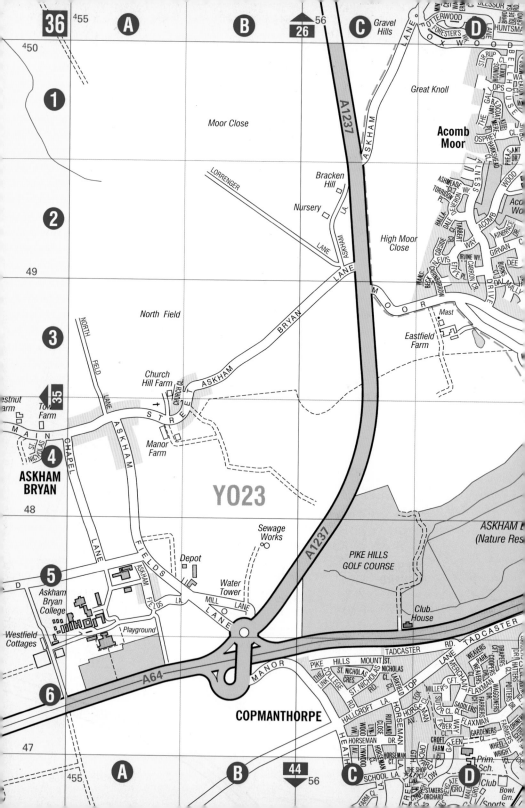

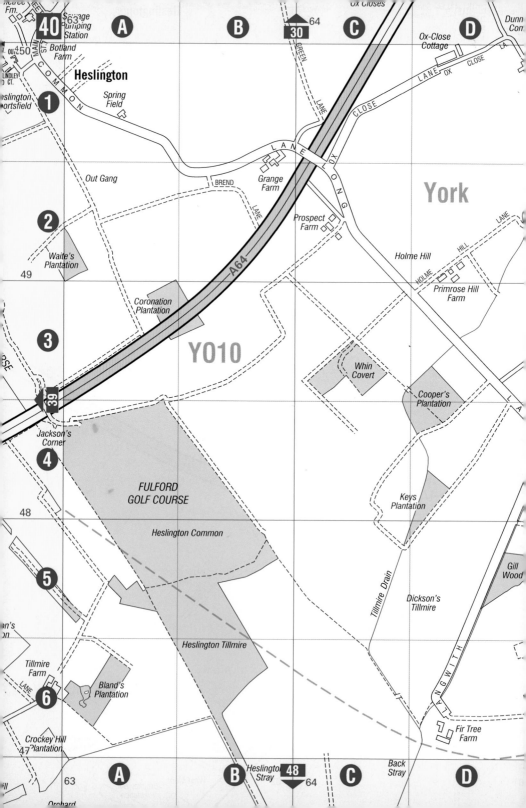

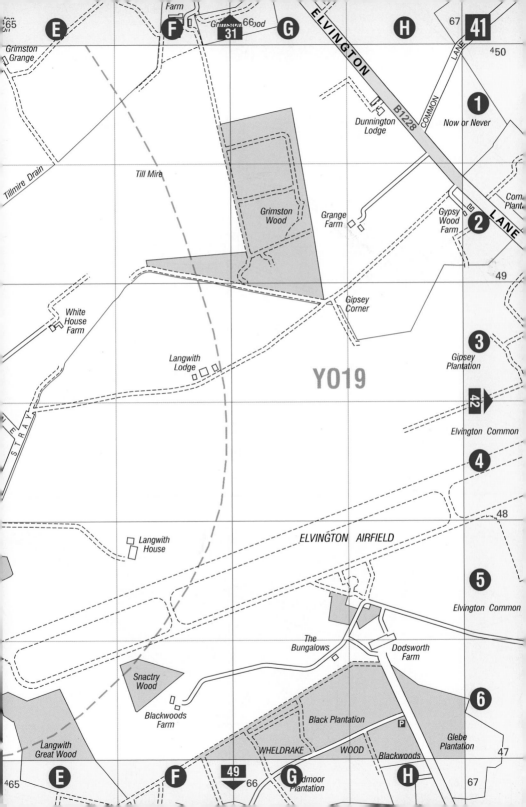

E 465

Grimston
Grange

Tillmire Drain

Till Mire

F Farm

Grimston 66ood

31

Grimston
Wood

White
House
Farm

Langwith
Lodge

G

Grange
Farm

Gipsey
Corner

ELVINGTON

Dunnington
Lodge

B1228

H

Now or Never

41

1

450

Gypsy
Wood
Farm

2

49

3

Gipsey
Plantation

42

Com.
Plant.

LANE

COMMON

67

YO19

STRAY

Langwith
House

Snactry
Wood

Blackwoods
Farm

E 465

Langwith
Great Wood

F

The
Bungalows

Elvington Common

4

48

ELVINGTON AIRFIELD

5

Elvington Common

Dodsworth
Farm

49 66

WHELDRAKE

Black Plantation

P

WOOD

G dmoor
Plantation

6

Glebe
Plantation

Blackwoods

H

47

67

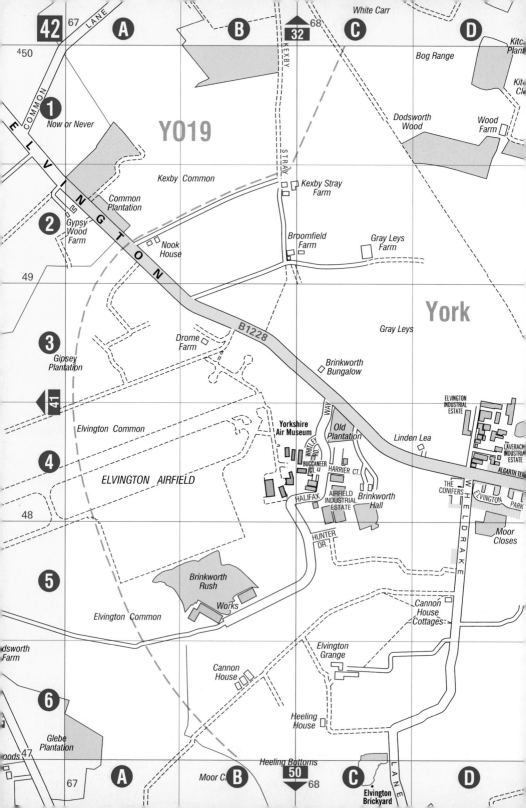

450

White Carr

Kitc...
Plan...

Bog Range

1
Now or Never

YO19

Dodsworth
Wood

Kit
Cl

Wood
Farm

Kexby Common

Common
Plantation

Kexby Stray
Farm

2
Gypsy
Wood
Farm

Nook
House

Broomfield
Farm

Gray Leys
Farm

49

B1228

York

3
Gipsey
Plantation

Drome
Farm

Brinkworth
Bungalow

Gray Leys

◄ 41

Elvington Common

WAY

ELVINGTON
INDUSTRIAL
ESTATE

4
ELVINGTON AIRFIELD

Yorkshire
Air Museum

WHITLEY RD

BUCCANEER
CT. U

Old
Plantation

Linden Lea

LAVERACK
INDUSTRIAL
ESTATE

ALGARTH TER

HARRIER CT.

HALIFAX

AIRFIELD
INDUSTRIAL
ESTATE

Brinkworth
Hall

THE
CONIFERS

ELVINGTON
PARK

48

5
Brinkworth
Rush

HUNTER
DR.

Moor
Closes

WHELDRAKE

Elvington Common

Works

Cannon
House
Cottages

dsworth
Farm

Elvington
Grange

Cannon
House

6
Glebe
Plantation

Heeling
House

oods
47

Heeling Bottoms

LANE

Elvington
Brickyard

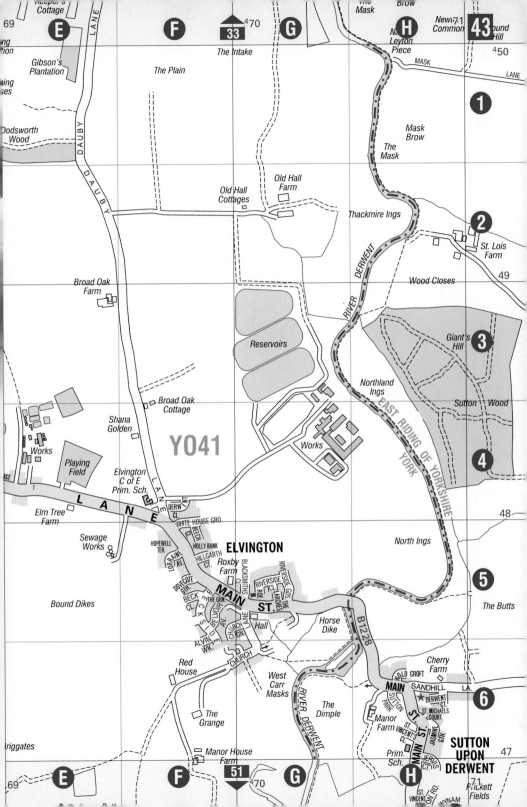

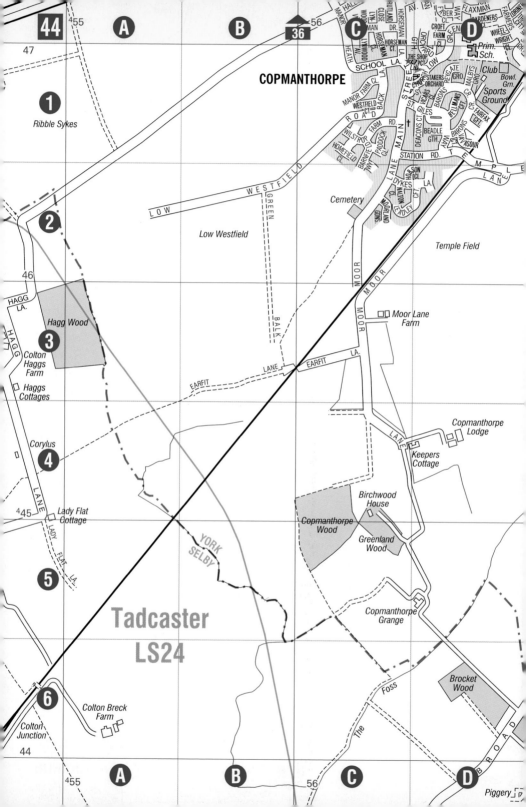

44 455

47

A   B   36 56   C   D

COPMANTHORPE

Prim. Sch.

Club

Bowl. Grn.

Sports Ground

1 Ribble Sykes

MANOR FARM CL.
WESTFIELD CT.
WILSTROP FARM RD.
HOMEFIELD CL.
BARNFIELD CL.
PADDOCK CL.

SCHOOL LA.
HEATH
ROAD
STREET
MAIN
STATION RD.

VICARS GTH.
DEACONS CT.
BEADLE GTH.
BELLMANS CGT.
BROWNS GRO.
FAIRFAX CGT.

2 46

LOW   WESTFIELD   ROAD

Low Westfield

GREEN

BALK

Cemetery

Temple Field

HAGG LA.

Hagg Wood

3 Colton Haggs Farm

Haggs Cottages

MOOR   LANE

Moor Lane Farm

EARFIT   LANE   EARFIT   LA.

EARFIT

Copmanthorpe Lodge

4 Corylus

LANE

Keepers Cottage

HAGG   LANE

Birchwood House

Copmanthorpe Wood

Greenland Wood

445

Lady Flat Cottage

LADY   FLAT   LA.

5

YORK SELBY

Copmanthorpe Grange

**Tadcaster
LS24**

6

Colton Junction

Colton Breck Farm

Brocket Wood

The   Foss

44

455

BROAD   ROAD

A   B   56   C   D

Piggery

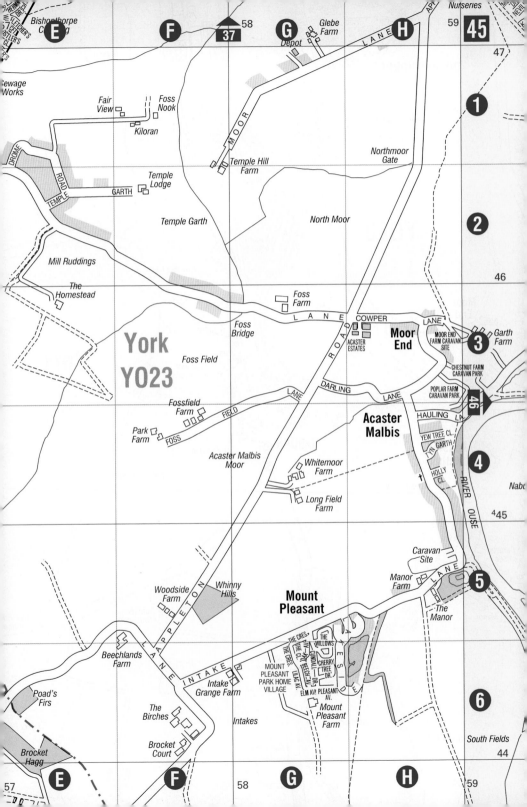

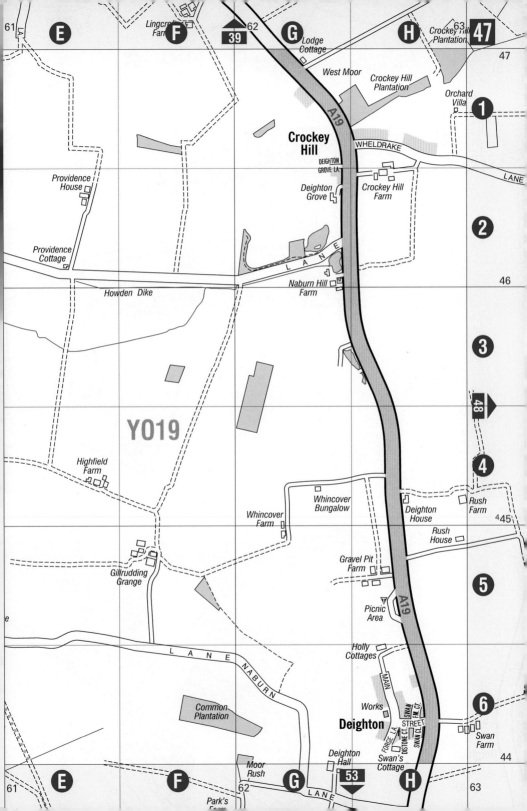

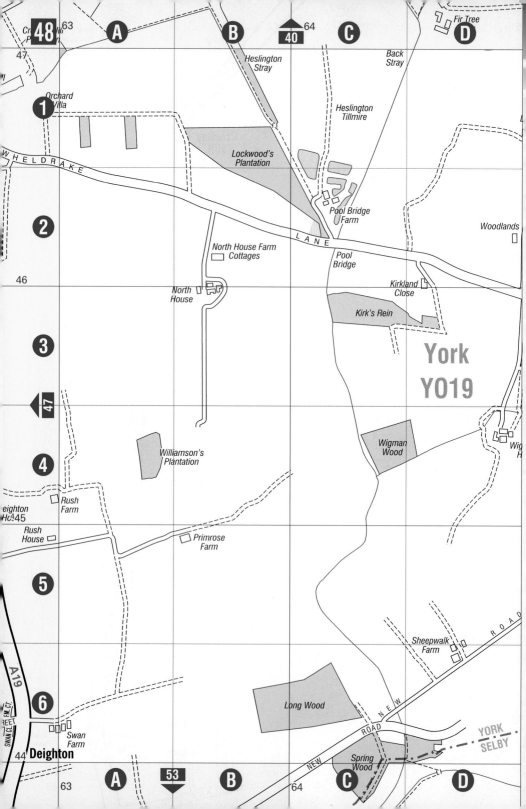

48

63 · 47 · 46 · 45 · 44 · 63 · 64

A · B · ▲40 64 · C · D Fir Tree

1 Orchard Villa

Heslington Stray

Back Stray

Heslington Tillmire

W H E L D R A K E

Lockwood's Plantation

Pool Bridge Farm

Woodlands

2

North House Farm Cottages

L A N E

Pool Bridge

North House

Kirkland Close

Kirk's Rein

3

York YO19

◀47

Williamson's Plantation

Wigman Wood

Wig H

4

eighton Ho

Rush Farm

Rush House

Primrose Farm

5

R O A D

Sheepwalk Farm

A19

6

Swan Farm

Deighton

Long Wood

N E W

R O A D

YORK SELBY

Spring Wood

A · ▼53 B · 64 · C · D

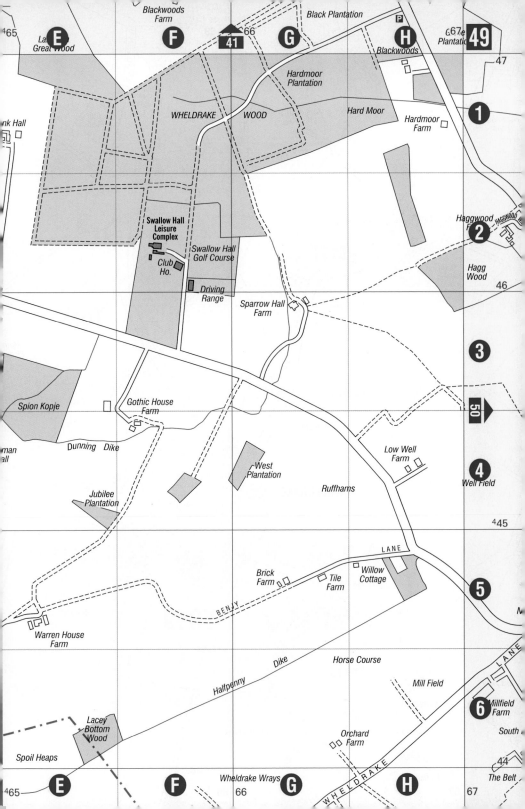

Plantation

52 ⁴60   **A**   Wood   Dike   **B**   Birker Plain   61   **C**   **47**   **D**

46

44   Halfpe Hill

Wood End Farm

1   Bell Hall

Naburn Wood   Park's Farm

Moreby Lodge

Birkhill Farm

2   Moreby

Mauds Ridding

Keeper's Cottage

Woodlands Farm

43

B1222

Moreby Park

The Gardens   Holly Dene

Moreby Wood

3

Moreby Far Wood

4   Stillingfleet   Beck

Wood House Farm

⁴42

Beck Farm

ROAD STILLINGFLEET   Escrick Grange Farm

5   Stillingfleet Hill

Reservoir (covered)

Post Office Radio Station   Hill Farm

Viewlands

Stillingfleet Grange

Stillingfleet Moor

6   Heron Wood

41

ESCRICK

⁴60   **A**   Longlands Plantation   **B**   61   **C**   **D**

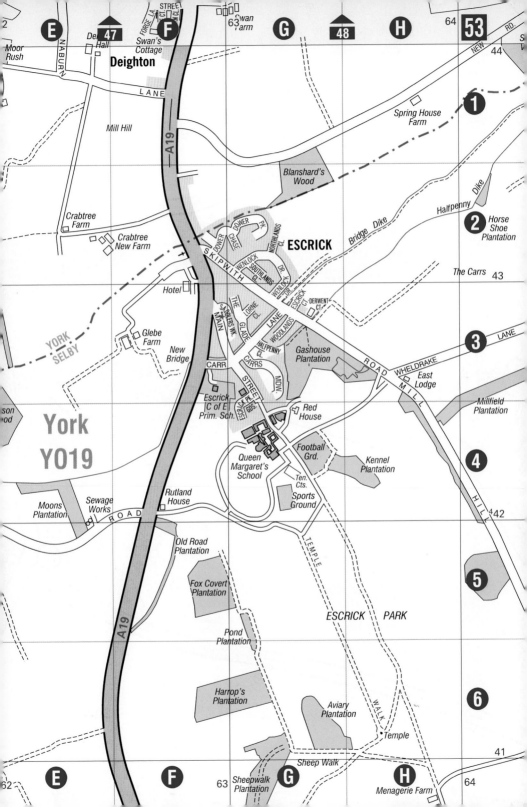

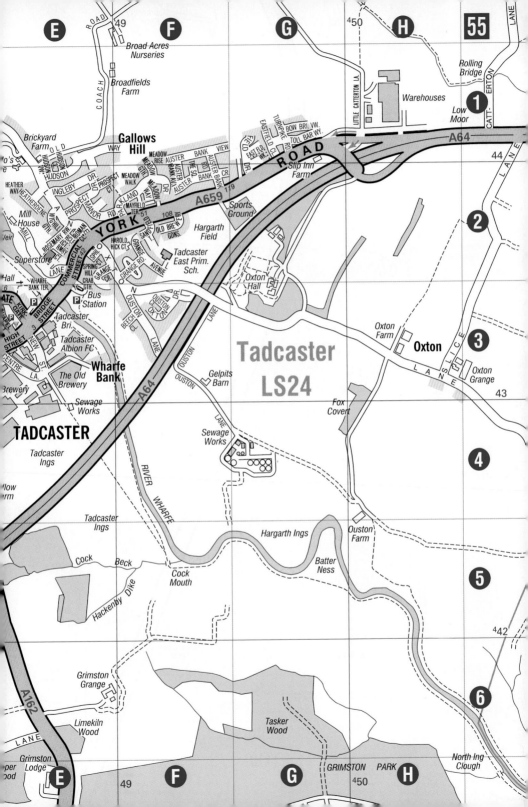

Grid references (top): E, F, G, H, 55

Grid references (right): 1, 2, 3, 4, 5, 6

Grid references (bottom): E, F, G, H

Map labels:

- ROAD
- 49
- Broad Acres Nurseries
- Broadfields Farm
- 450
- Rolling Bridge
- Warehouses
- LITTLE CATTERTON LA.
- Low Moor
- CATTERTON LANE
- Brickyard Farm
- Gallows Hill
- COACH WAY
- HUDSON DR.
- OLD HUDSON
- MEADOW RISE
- MEADOW WALK
- MEADOW BANK
- AUSTER BANK RD.
- AUSTER BANK
- THE SQ.
- AUSTER BANK CR.
- AUSTER BANK AV.
- AUSTER BANK VIEW
- EASTFIELD DR.
- EAST FLD.
- TURNPIKE RD.
- BOW BRI. VW.
- TOLL BAR WY.
- ROAD
- Slip Inn Farm
- A64
- 44
- HEATHER WAY
- HEATHERDENE
- WIGHILL
- INGLEBY
- PROSPECT CT.
- MANOR DR.
- MEADOW CRFT.
- PARKLAND DR.
- MAYFIELD TER.
- OLD BREW
- A659
- 119
- Sports Ground
- Mill House
- MILL
- ROSEMARY RW.
- SPRINGS
- COMMERCIAL STREET
- HAROLD HICK CT.
- ROMAN RD.
- 108
- SANDY
- GRANGE GDNS.
- Hargarth Field
- Tadcaster East Prim. Sch.
- Oxton Hall
- Oxton Farm
- Oxton
- Oxton Grange
- 43
- Superstore
- Hall
- WHARFE BANK TER.
- BRIDGE STREET
- Bus Station
- Tadcaster Bri.
- Tadcaster Albion FC
- SPRINGS HILL
- GRANGE RD.
- OUSTON CL.
- OUSTON DR.
- BEECH CL.
- OUSTON LANE
- AVENUE
- SLICE LANE
- HIGH STREET
- NEW ST.
- CENTRE
- GATE
- The Old Brewery
- Wharfe Bank
- Brewery
- Sewage Works
- Gelpits Barn
- A64
- OUSTON LANE
- Tadcaster LS24
- Fox Covert
- TADCASTER
- Tadcaster Ings
- Sewage Works
- Tadcaster Ings
- low rm
- RIVER WHARFE
- Hargarth Ings
- Ouston Farm
- Batter Ness
- Cock Beck
- Cock Mouth
- Hackenby Dike
- 42
- Grimston Grange
- A162 LANE
- Limekiln Wood
- Tasker Wood
- Grimston Lodge
- per ood
- 49
- GRIMSTON PARK
- 450
- North Ing Clough

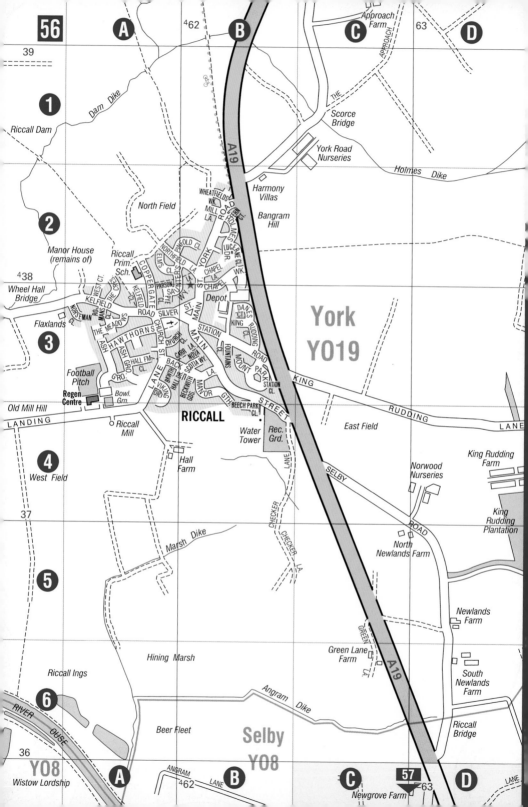

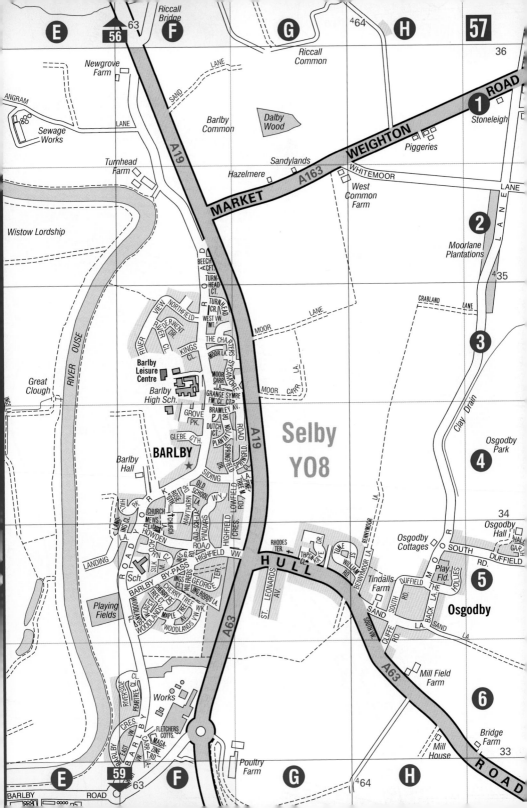

Selby YO8

BARLBY

Osgodby

Labels and place names

E · 56 · Riccall Bridge · F · G · 464 · H · 57 · 36

Newgrove Farm

ANGRAM

Sewage Works

LANE

Riccall Common

Barlby Common

Dalby Wood

WEIGHTON ROAD · 1 · Stoneleigh

Turnhead Farm

MARKET · A163 · WHITEMOOR · Piggeries

Hazelmere · Sandylands

Wistow Lordship

West Common Farm

LANE · 2 · 435

A19

BEECH CFT.
TURNHEAD CT.
TURNHEAD CR.
WEST VW. MT.
VIEW · NORTHFIELD
RIVER DR. · DERWENT CL.
KINGS CL.
THE CHARTERS
MOOR LA.
SYCAMORE
MOOR CARR LA.
GRANGE SYMRE FM. CL. CT.
BRAMLEY AV.
DUTCH CT.
PLANT LA.

Moorlane Plantations

CRABLAND LANE

LANE

MOOR · CARR

3

River Ouse

Great Clough

Barlby Leisure Centre

Barlby High Sch.

GROVE PK.

GLEBE GTH.

Clay Drain

Osgodby Park

4

Barlby Hall

LANDING

CHURCH MEWS
HOWDEN
CHURCH
SILK
PINDARS
GEORGE TER.
HIGHFIELD CRES.
OLD SCHOOL LA.
HAWTHORN DR.
ROSE GTH.
SPRINGFIELD DR.
SIDING
LOWFIELD
PINE TREE LA.
A19
ROAD

34

Osgodby Cottages

Osgodby Hall · HALL · GAR.

SOUTH · DUFFIELD RD.

5

RHODES TER.
THOS. DVE. CL.
TUNE RD.
WILLIAM ST.
BENNYMOOR LA.

Tindalls Farm

DUFFIELD RD.
THE HOLLIES

SAND · LA. · BACK LA. · SAND LA.

Osgodby

Playing Fields

SCH.
BY-PASS
LONG ROODS LA.
WILFREDS
CHERRY TREE
MAPLE
WOODLANDS WK.
BARLBY
RIVERSIDE CL.
PEARTREE CL.
EAST CRES.
BARLBY
FLETCHERS COTTS.
MAGAZINE
CARR RD.

Works

Mill Field Farm

6

A63 · HULL · ST. LEONARDS AV. · CLIFFE RD. · SOUTH VW.

Poultry Farm

Mill House

Bridge Farm · 33

E · 59 · 63 · F · G · 464 · H · ROAD

BARLBY ROAD

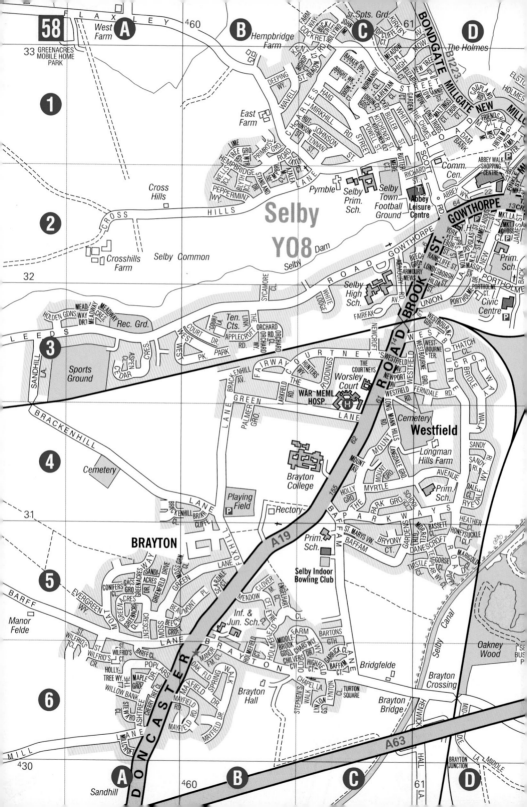

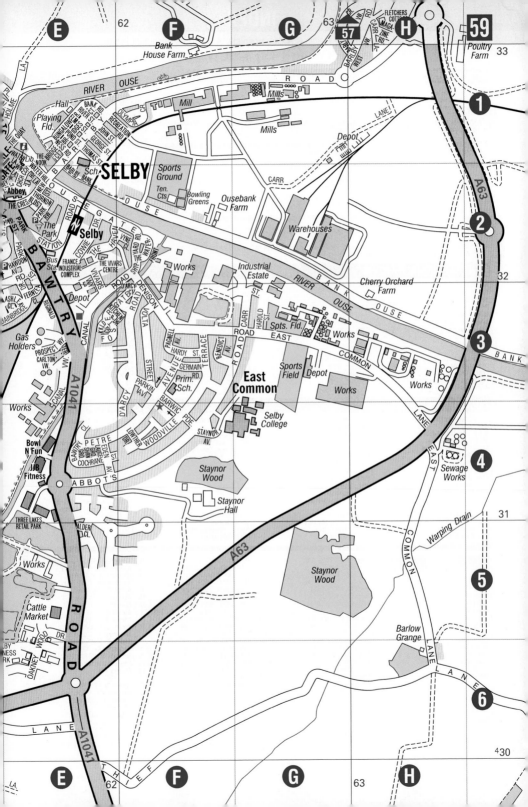

INDEX

Including Streets, Places & Areas, Hospitals & Hospices, Industrial Estates,
Selected Flats & Walkways, Stations and Selected Places of Interest.

HOW TO USE THIS INDEX

1. Each street name is followed by its Postcode District, then by its Locality abbreviation(s) and then by its map reference;
e.g. **Abbot's Rd.** YO8: Sel . . . .**4E 59** is in the YO8 Postcode District and the Selby Locality and is to be found in square 4E on page **59**.
The page number is shown in bold type.

2. A strict alphabetical order is followed in which Av., Rd., St., etc. (though abbreviated) are read in full and as part of the street name;
e.g. **Foxcroft** appears after **Fox Covert** but before **Fox Gth.**

3. Streets and a selection of flats and walkways too small to be shown on the maps, appear in the index with the thoroughfare to which it is connected shown in brackets; e.g. **Aberford Ho.** YO31: York . . . .1D **28** (off Lowther St.)

4. Addresses that are in more than one part are referred to as not continuous.

5. Places and areas are shown in the index in BLUE TYPE and the map reference is to the actual map square in which the town centre or area is located and not to the place name shown on the map; e.g. **ACOMB** 4E **27**

6. An example of a selected place of interest is Selby Abbey 2E **59**

7. An example of a station is **Poppleton Station (Rail)** . . . .5B **16**. Included are Rail **(Rail)** and Park & Ride

8. An example of a hospital or hospice is BOOTHAM PARK HOSPITAL 1C **28**

9. Map references for entries that appear on large scale pages **2** & **3** are shown first, with small scale map references shown in brackets;
e.g. **Agar St.** YO31: York 1G **3** (2D **28**)

GENERAL ABBREVIATIONS

Av. : Avenue	**Cft.** : Croft	**La.** : Lane	**Ri.** : Rise
Bk. : Back	**Dr.** : Drive	**Lit.** : Little	**Rd.** : Road
Blvd. : Boulevard	**E.** : East	**Lwr.** : Lower	**Shop.** : Shopping
Bri. : Bridge	**Est.** : Estate	**Mnr.** : Manor	**Sth.** : South
Bldgs. : Buildings	**Fld.** : Field	**Mkt.** : Market	**Sq.** : Square
Bungs. : Bungalows	**Flds.** : Fields	**Mdw.** : Meadow	**St.** : Street
Bus. : Business	**Gdns.** : Gardens	**Mdws.** : Meadows	**Ter.** : Terrace
Cvn. : Caravan	**Gth.** : Garth	**M.** : Mews	**Trad.** : Trading
Cen. : Centre	**Ga.** : Gate	**Mt.** : Mount	**Up.** : Upper
Cl. : Close	**Grn.** : Green	**Mus.** : Museum	**Va.** : Vale
Comn. : Common	**Gro.** : Grove	**Nth.** : North	**Vw.** : View
Cott. : Cottage	**Hgts.** : Heights	**Pde.** : Parade	**Vs.** : Villas
Cotts. : Cottages	**Ho.** : House	**Pk.** : Park	**Wlk.** : Walk
Ct. : Court	**Ind.** : Industrial	**Pas.** : Passage	**W.** : West
Cres. : Crescent	**Info.** : Information	**Pl.** : Place	**Yd.** : Yard

LOCALITY ABBREVIATIONS

Aca M : **Acaster Malbis**	Esc : **Escrick**	Moor M : **Moor Monkton**	Stock F : **Stockton-on-the-Forest**
Ang : **Angram**	Flax : **Flaxton**	Mur : **Murton**	Stre : **Strensall**
App R : **Appleton Roebuck**	Ful : **Fulford**	Nab : **Naburn**	Stut : **Stutton**
Ask B : **Askham Bryan**	Gate H : **Gate Helmsley**	Neth P : **Nether Poppleton**	Sutt F : **Sutton-on-the-Forest**
Ask R : **Askham Richard**	Grim : **Grimston**	New E : **New Earswick**	Sutt D : **Sutton upon Derwent**
B'by : **Barlby**	Hax : **Haxby**	Newt K : **Newton Kyme**	Tad : **Tadcaster**
B'lw : **Barlow**	Heal : **Healaugh**	Osb : **Osbaldwick**	Thor : **Thorganby**
Bilb : **Bilbrough**	H'tn : **Heslington**	Osg : **Osgodby**	Tow : **Towthorpe**
Bish : **Bishopthorpe**	Hess : **Hessay**	Over : **Overton**	Up P : **Upper Poppleton**
Bray : **Brayton**	Holt : **Holtby**	Oxt : **Oxton**	W'hil : **Warthill**
Col : **Colton**	Hunt : **Huntington**	Ric : **Riccall**	Whel : **Wheldrake**
Cop : **Copmanthorpe**	Hut W : **Hutton Wandesley**	Ruff : **Rufforth**	Wigg : **Wigginton**
Crock H : **Crockey Hill**	Kex : **Kexby**	Sel : **Selby**	Wist L : **Wistow Lordship**
Dei : **Deighton**	Knap : **Knapton**	Ship : **Shipton**	York : **York**
Dun : **Dunnington**	Long M : **Long Marston**	Ske : **Skelton**	
Ear : **Earswick**	Low C : **Low Catton**	Stam B : **Stamford Bridge**	
Elv : **Elvington**	Mid : **Middlethorpe**	Still : **Stillingfleet**	

A

	Acomb Wood Shop. Cen.	Alder Cl. YO8: Sel 5E 59	Almery Ter. YO30: York 2B **2** (2B **28**)
Abbey Leisure Cen. 2D 58	YO24: York 2E 37	Alderley Ct. YO32: Hunt 2E 19	Almond Gro. YO32: New E 1D 18
Abbey Pl. YO8: Sel 2E 59	Acorn ARL Sports & Social Club	Aldersyde YO24: York 2G 37	Almsford Dr. YO26: York 2D 26
Abbey St. YO30: York 6A 18	. . . . .6F 27	Aldersyde Ct. YO24: York 2G 37	Almsford Rd. YO26: York 2D 26
Abbey Wlk. YO8: Sel 2D 58	Acorn Cl. YO8: B'by 5F 57	Aldersyde M. YO24: York 2G 37	Alness Dr. YO24: York 2D 36
Abbey Wlk. Shop. Cen.	Acorn Way YO24: York 1F 37	Aldreth Gro. YO23: York 5C 28	Alne Ter. YO10: York 6H **3** (5E **29**)
YO8: Sel 1D 58	Adbrough Ho. YO31: York 1C **28**	Aldwark YO1: York 2F **3** (2D **28**)	Alvin Wlk. YO41: Elv 6F 43
Abbey Yd. YO8: Sel 2D 58	(off Brook St.)	Alexa Cl. YO24: York 4E 27	Alvis Gro. YO10: Osb 3B 30
Abbotsford Rd. YO10: York 4F 29	Adelaide St. YO23: York 5B 28	Alexander Av. YO31: York 3E 19	Alwyne Dr. YO30: York 4G 17
Abbots Gait YO32: Hunt 5F 11	Adlington Cl. YO32: Stre 4H 5	Alexandra Ct.	Alwyne Gro. YO30: York 4G 17
Abbot's Rd. YO8: Sel 4E 59	Ainsty Av. YO24: York 1H 37	YO10: York 4H **3** (3E **29**)	Amberley St. YO26: York 2C 27
Abbot St. YO31: York 1D 28	Ainsty Ct. YO10: H'tn 1H 39	Alexandra Rd. YO32: Stre 6H 5	Amber St. YO31: York 1D 28
Abbotsway YO31: York 5E 19	Ainsty Gro. YO24: York 1H 37	Alex Lyon Ho. YO31: York 3F 29	Ambleside Av. YO10: York 3H 29
Abelton Gro. YO32: Hax 2D 10	Ainsty Rd. YO24: York 1H 37	Algarth Ri. YO31: York 6H 19	Ambrose St. YO10: York 6D 28
Aberford Ho. YO31: York 1D **28**	Airfield Ind. Est. YO41: Elv 4C 42	Algarth Rd. YO31: York 6H 19	Amy Johnson Way YO30: York . . .2A 18
(off Lowther St.)	Albany St. YO26: York 2H 27	Algarth Ter. YO41: Elv 4D 42	Ancress Wlk.
Acacia Av. YO32: New E 1E 19	Albemarle Rd.	Allanson Gro. YO24: York 5G 27	YO23: York 6D **2** (4B **28**)
Acacia Gro. YO32: Hax 2D 10	. . . . .6A **2** (5A **28**)	Allan St. YO30: York 6C 18	Ancroft Cl. YO1: York 5F **3** (4D **28**)
Acaster Estates	Albert Cl. YO24: York 5E 27	Allen Cl. YO10: York 3G 29	Anderson Gro. YO24: York 5H 27
YO23: Aca M 3H 45	YO32: Hunt 5F 19	Allendale YO24: York 1F 37	Andrew Dr. YO32: Hunt 4F 19
Acaster La. YO23: Aca M, Bish . . .1B 46	Albert St. YO10: York 5G **3** (4D **28**)	Allerton Dr.	ANGRAM 3B 34
ACASTER MALBIS 4H 45	Albion Av. YO26: York 1D 26	YO26: Neth P, Up P 3B 16	Angram La. YO8: B'by . . .6B **56** & 1E **57**
ACOMB MOOR 1D 36	Albion St. YO1: York 5G **3** (5D **28**)	Allington Dr. YO31: York 1H 29	Annam Cl. YO24: York 3E 37
Acomb Rd. YO24: York 4F 27	Alcelina Ct. YO23: York 6D **2** (4C **28**)	All Saints La. YO1: York 3D **2**	Anne St. YO23: York 5C 28
Acomb Wood Cl. YO24: York 1E 37	Alcuin Av. YO10: York 3F 29	Alma Cl. YO10: York 5D 28	Ann Harrison's Almshouses
Acomb Wood Dr. YO24: York 2D 36	Alcuin Way YO10: H'tn 5H 29	Alma Gro. YO10: York 5D 28	YO31: York 1D **28**
	Aldborough Way	Alma Ter. YO8: Sel 1D 58	(off Penley's Gro. St.)
	YO26: York 2A **2** (2H **27**)	YO10: York 5D 28	Annie St. YO8: Sel 1D 58

Anson Dr.—Brecks La.

Anson Dr. YO10: York 1D 38
Anthea Dr. YO31: York 4E 19
Apollo Ct. YO10: York 6H 3 (4E 29)
Apollo St. YO10: York 6H 3 (4E 29)
Appleby Glade YO32: Hax 4D 10
Appleby Pl. YO31: York 2G 29
Applecroft Rd. YO8: Sel 3B 58
YO31: York 6H 19
Apple Gth. YO26: Up P 4B 16
Appleton Ct. YO23: Bish 6H 37
Appleton Rd. YO23: Aca M 5F 45
YO23: Bish 6H 37
Appletree Wlk. YO26: Tad 5C 54
Approach, The YO19: Esc 1C 56
Arbor Cl. YO32: Hunt 2E 19
Archway, The
YO31: York 2H 3 (2E 29)
Ardsley Ho. *YO31: York 1D 28*
(off Del Pyke)
Arenhall Cl. YO32: Wigg 3C 10
Argyle St. YO23: York 6B 28
Arlington Rd. YO30: York 4A 18
Armoury M. YO8: Sel 2C 58
Armoury Rd. YO8: Sel 2C 58
Armstrong Way YO30: York 2G 17
Arncliffe Ho. *YO26: York 3G 27*
(off Burnsall Dr.)
Arncliffe M. *YO10: York 5D 28*
(off Alma Ter.)
Arndale Ct. YO24: York 6H 27
Arnside Pl. YO10: York 4F 29
Arran Pl. YO31: York 6D 18
Arthur Pl. YO30: Ske 6D 8
Arthur St. YO10: York 4E 29
Artspace, The . . . . *5E 3 (3C 28)*
(off Tower St.)
Arundel Gro. YO24: York 2E 37
Ascot Rd. YO24: York 5F 27
YO32: Wigg 1B 10
Ascot Way YO24: York 6F 27
Ashbourne Pl. YO24: York 2E 37
Ashbourne Way YO24: York 1E 37
Ash Cl. YO31: York 6H 19
Ashdale Rd. YO19: Dun 2A 32
Ashfield Ct. YO24: York 2G 37
Ashfield Touring Cvn. Pk.
YO19: Dun 3B 32
Ashford Pl. YO24: York 5F 27
Ash Gro. YO19: Ric 3A 56
Ash Ho. YO23: York 1C 38
Ash La. YO32: Hax 1D 10
Ashlea Cl. YO8: Sel 3E 59
Ashley Pk. Cres. YO31: York 1H 29
Ashley Pk. Rd. YO31: York 6H 19
Ashmeade Cl. YO24: York 2D 36
Ash St. YO26: York 2G 27
Ashton Av. YO30: York 5B 18
Ashtree Dr. YO8: Bray 6A 58
Ashtree Wlk. YO26: Tad 5C 54
Ashville St. YO31: York 6D 18
Ash Wlk. YO32: Stre 4A 6
Ashwood Glade YO32: Hax 5C 10
Askham Bog (Nature Reserve) . . .5D 36
ASKHAM BRYAN 4A 36
Askham Bryan La. YO23: Ask B . . .3B 36
Askham Cft. YO24: York 6D 26
Askham Flds. La. YO23: Ask B . . .4A 36
(not continuous)
Askham Gro. YO24: York 5D 26
Askham La. YO23: Ask B 2C 36
YO24: York 1C 36
ASKHAM RICHARD 5F 35
Askrigg Ho. *YO26: York 3G 27*
(off Bouthwaite Dr.)
Aspen Cl. YO8: Sel 3A 58
YO19: Dun 1A 32
Aspen Way YO26: Tad 3C 54
Asquith Av. YO31: York 2G 29
Aston Ho. YO24: York 6G 27
Atcherley Cl. YO10: York 1D 38
Atlas Rd. YO30: York 2A 18
Atterwith La. YO26: Hess 6A 14
Aucuba Cl. YO32: New E 3D 18
Audax Cl. YO30: York 2A 18
Audax Ct. YO30: York 2A 18
Audax Rd. YO30: York 2A 18
Audus St. YO8: Sel 2D 58
Auster Bank Av. YO26: Tad 2F 55
Auster Bank Cres. YO26: Tad 2F 55
Auster Bank Rd. YO26: Tad 1F 55
Auster Bank Vw. YO26: Tad 1F 55
Auster Rd. YO30: York 2B 18
Authitts Cotts. YO30: Ship 2A 8
Avenue, The YO23: Ruff 4D 24
YO30: York 1A 28
YO32: Hax 3D 10
(Park Est.)
YO32: Hax 1C 10
(Southlands)
Avenue Rd. YO30: York 1B 28
Avenue Ter. YO30: York 1B 28
Aviator Ct. YO30: York 2H 17
Avon Dr. YO32: Hunt 5F 11
Avon Ho. YO10: York 5G 3
Aylesham Ct. YO32: Hunt 2E 19
Aysgarth Ho. *YO26: York 3G 27*
(off Bouthwaite Dr.)
Ayton Ho. *YO31: York 1C 28*
(off Cole St.)
Azalea M. YO8: Sel 2B 58

B

Bacchus Ho. *YO10: York 3F 29*
(off Olympian Ct.)
Bachelor Hill YO24: York 5E 27
Backhouse St. YO31: York 1C 28
Back La. YO8: Osg 5H 57
YO19: Dun, Holt 6H 21
YO19: Ric 3A 56
YO23: Cop 1C 44
YO26: Knap 2C 26
YO32: Wigg 2B 10
Back La. Sth. YO19: Whel 5B 50
Back St. YO8: Sel 2D 58
Back Swinegate
YO1: York 3E 3 (3C 28)
Bad Bargain La. YO31: York 2G 29
Badger Paddock YO31: York 3E 19
Badgerwood Wlk YO10: York 5A 30
Baffam Ct. YO8: Bray 6C 58
Baffam Gdns. YO8: Sel 5C 58
Baffam La. YO8: Sel 4C 58
Baildon Cl. YO26: York 3F 27
Baile Hill Ter. YO1: York . . .6D 2 (4C 28)
Bainbridge Dr. YO8: Sel 3E 59
Baker St. YO30: York 6C 18
Balfour St. YO26: York 2H 27
Balfour Way YO32: Stre 5H 5
Balmoral Ter. YO23: York 6B 28
Bank Rd. YO8: Sel 1E 59
Bankside Cl. YO26: Up P 3B 16
Bannisdale YO24: York 2E 37
Barbara Gro. YO24: York 4H 27
Barbers Dr. YO23: Cop 6D 36
Barbican Ct. YO10: York 6G 3 (4D 28)
Barbican M. YO10: York . . .5H 3 (4E 29)
Barbican Rd.
YO10: York 6G 3 (4D 28)
Bar Convent Mus., The . . .5B 2 (4B 28)
Barden Ct. YO30: York 4H 17
Barff Cl. YO8: Bray 6A 58
Barff La. YO8: Bray 5A 58
Barfield Rd. YO31: York 5F 19
Barker Dr. YO8: Sel 1C 58
Barker La. YO1: York 4C 2 (3B 28)
Barkston Av. YO26: York 4C 26
Barkston Cl. YO26: York 4C 26
Barkston Gro. YO26: York 4C 26
Barkston Rd. YO26: York 4C 26
Bar La. YO1: York 4B 2 (3B 28)
BARLBY .4F 57
Barlby Bank YO8: Sel 2E 59
Barlby By-Pass YO8: B'by 5F 57
Barlby Cres. YO8: Sel 6E 57
Barlby Leisure Cen. 3F 57
Barlby Rd. YO8: B'by, Sel 1H 59
YO8: Sel 1E 59
Barleycorn Yd.
YO1: York 4F 3 (3D 28)
Barley Hall 2E 3
Barley Ri. YO32: Stre 5H 5
Barley Vw. YO32: Hax, Wigg 3C 10
Barlow St. YO26: York 3F 27
Barmby Av. YO10: York 1E 39
Barmby Cl. YO30: York 4H 17
Barnfield Way YO23: Cop 1C 44
Barn Gro. YO10: H'tn 6G 29
Baron Glade YO30: York 5G 17
Barons Cres. YO23: Cop 1D 44
Barrett Av. YO24: York 4H 27
Barr La. YO32: Stock F 4F 13
Barstow Av. YO10: York 4F 29
Bartle Gth. YO1: York 2F 3 (2D 28)
Barton Cl. YO30: York 3G 17
Bartons Gth. YO8: Sel 5C 58
Barwic Pde. YO8: Sel 3F 59
Bassett Cl. YO8: Sel 5D 58
Bateson Cl. YO10: H'tn 6A 30
Battleflats Way YO41: Stam B 4H 23
Bawtry Cl. YO8: Sel 4E 59
Bawtry Rd. YO8: Sel 2E 59
Baysdale Av. YO10: Osb 3B 30
Beaconsfield M. YO24: York 4F 27
Beaconsfield St. YO24: York 4F 27
Beadle Gth. YO23: Cop 1D 44
Beagle Cft. YO41: Stam B 3H 23
Beagle Ridge Dr. YO24: York 6E 27
Beagle Spinney YO41: Stam B 3H 23
Bean's Way YO31: York 5H 19
Beaufort Cl. YO10: York 4H 29
Beaulieu Cl. YO32: Hunt 6F 11
Beaumont Pl. YO8: Bray 5A 58
Beaverdyke YO30: York 4H 17
Beck Cl. YO41: Elv 5F 43
Beckett Dr. YO10: Osb 3B 30
Beckfield La. YO26: York 3D 26
Beckfield Pl. YO26: York 3D 26
Beck La. YO19: Whel 4C 50
Beckside YO41: Elv 5F 43
Beckside Gdns. YO10: York 3F 29
Beckwith Cl. YO31: York 6A 20
Beckwith Gdns. YO19: Ric 3B 56
Beckwith Hall Dr. YO19: Ric 3A 56
Bedale Av. YO10: Osb 3B 30
Bedale Ho. *YO31: York 1D 28*
(off Townend St.)
Bede Av. YO30: York 6B 18
Bedern YO1: York 2F 3 (2D 28)
Bedford M. YO30: York 1B 2
Beech Av. YO23: Aca M 6G 45
YO23: Bish 6A 38
YO24: York 4H 27
Beech Cl. YO26: Tad 3F 55
YO41: Elv 5F 43
Beech Cft. YO8: B'by 2F 57
Beechcroft YO8: Bray 5A 58
Beeches, The YO26: Up P 3B 16
YO30: Ske 1E 17
Beech Glade YO31: York 3F 19
Beech Gro. YO8: Sel 2C 58
YO26: Up P 4A 16
YO26: York 3E 27
Beech Pk. Cl. YO19: Ric 4B 56
Beech Pl. YO32: Stre 5H 5
Beechtree Rd. YO26: Tad 4C 54
Beech Wlk. YO26: Tad 3C 54
Beech Way YO26: Up P 4B 16
Beechway Cl. YO26: Up P 4B 16
Beechwood Glade YO24: York 6D 26
Beechwood Grange Cvn. Pk.
YO32: York 1B 20
Beeforth Cl. YO32: New E 6D 10
Belcombe Way YO30: York 6A 18
Belgrave St. YO31: York 6C 18
Bell Cl. YO32: Wigg 3C 10
Belle Vue St.
YO10: York 6H 3 (4E 29)
Belle Vue Ter.
YO10: York 6H 3 (4E 29)
Bellfarm Av. YO31: York 5E 19
Bellhouse Way YO24: York 1D 36
Bellmans Cft. YO23: Cop 1D 44
Bellwood Dr. YO24: York 1E 37
Belmont Cl. YO30: York 4H 17
Belvoir Av. YO41: Elv 5F 43
Bempton Ho. *YO31: York 1D 28*
(off Del Pyke)
Benedict Av. YO8: Sel 3F 59
Benjy La. YO19: Whel 5F 49
Bennymoor La. YO8: Osg 5H 57
Bentham Ho. *YO26: York 3G 27*
(off Burnsall Dr.)
Bentley Pk. YO10: Osb 3B 30
Beresford Ter. YO23: York 6C 28
Berkeley Ho. *YO10: York 4F 29*
(off Milton St.)
Berkeley Ter. YO26: York 2G 27
Beverley Balk YO41: Gate H 1D 22
Beverley Ct. YO24: York 6F 27
Beverley Gdns. YO31: York 1E 29
Bewlay St. YO23: York 5C 28
Bilsdale Cl. YO30: York 3G 17
Birch Cl. YO32: New E 2D 18
Birch Copse YO24: York 5F 27
Birch La. YO32: Hax 2D 10
Birch Pk. YO31: York 4E 19
Birch Pk. Ind. Est.
YO31: York 4E 19
Birch Tree Cl. YO32: Stre 5H 5
Birch Tree Ct. YO32: Hax 2D 10
Birkdale Gro. YO26: York 2D 26
Birstwith Dr. YO26: York 3G 27
Bishop Ct. YO8: Sel 1C 58
Bishopfields Cloisters
YO26: York 3A 2 (3A 28)
Bishopfields Dr. YO26: York 3A 28
Bishopgate St.
YO23: York 6D 2 (4C 28)
Bishophill Junior
YO1: York 5C 2 (4B 28)
Bishophill Senior
YO1: York 4D 2 (4C 28)
Bishops Ct. YO1: York 5D 2 (3C 28)
Bishops Way YO10: York 5A 30
BISHOPTHORPE 5A 38
Bishopthorpe Rd.
YO23: Bish, Mid, York
. . . . .6D 2 (5B 38)
Bismarck St. YO26: York 2H 27
Black Dike La. YO26: Up P 5A 16
Black Horse Pas. *YO1: York 3F 3*
(off Fossgate)
Blacklee Cl. YO32: Stre 2B 6
Blacksmiths Cl. YO41: Elv 5G 43
Blackthorn Dr. YO31: York 3E 19
Blake Ct. YO19: Whel 4C 50
Blakeley Gro. YO30: York 2H 17
Blakeney Pl. YO10: York 4F 29
Blake St. YO1: York 2D 2 (2C 28)
Bland La. YO26: Knap 3C 26
Blatchford Ct. YO30: York 5B 18
Blatchford M. *YO30: York 5B 18*
(off Tamworth Rd.)
Bleachfield YO10: H'tn 5F 29
Blenheim Ct. YO30: York 2F 17
Bleriot Way YO30: York 2A 18
Blossom St. YO24: York . . .5B 2 (4B 28)
Bluebeck Dr. YO30: York 5G 17
Blue Bri. La. YO10: York . . .6F 3 (5D 28)
Blue Coat YO19: Mur 1E 31
Blue Slates Cl. YO19: Whel 4D 50
Blyth Cl. YO8: Sel 2B 58
Board St. YO23: York 6E 3 (5C 28)
Bog La. YO24: York 3D 36
Boleyn Ho. *YO1: York 5E 3*
(off Lady Anne Ct.)
Bollans Ct. YO1: York 2F 3
Boltby Rd. YO30: York 3H 17
Bolton Ho. *YO10: York 4F 29*
(off Nicholas Gdns.)
Bondgate YO8: Sel 1D 58
Bonington Ct. YO26: York 3G 27
Bootham YO30: York 1C 2 (2B 28)
Bootham Cres. YO30: York 1B 28
Bootham Pk. Ct. YO30: York 1C 28
BOOTHAM PARK HOSPITAL 1C 28
Bootham Pl. YO30: York 1D 2
Bootham Row
YO30: York 1D 2 (2C 28)
Bootham Sq.
YO30: York 1D 2 (2C 28)
BOOTHAM STRAY 3A 18
Bootham Ter.
YO30: York 1B 2 (2B 28)
Boothwood Rd. YO30: York 3H 17
Bore Tree Baulk YO19: Grim 3E 31
Boroughbridge Rd. YO26: York . . .6D 16
Borrowdale Dr. YO30: York 4H 17
Borthwick Institute for Archives
. . . . .5G 29
Boss La. YO10: H'tn 6H 29
Bouthwaite Dr. YO26: York 3G 27
Bow Bri. Vw. YO26: Tad 1G 55
Bowes Av. YO31: York 2E 29
Bowland Way YO30: York 4A 18
Bowling Grn. Ct. YO31: York 5D 18
Bowling Grn. Cft. YO31: York 5D 18
Bowling Grn. La. YO31: York 1D 28
Bowl N Fun 4E 59
Bowness Dr. YO30: York 4G 17
Bowyers Cl. YO23: Cop 6E 37
Bracken Cl. YO32: Hunt 1F 19
Bracken Hill YO10: Osb 4A 30
Brackenhill Av. YO8: Sel 3B 58
Brackenhill Cl. YO8: Bray 4A 58
Brackenhill La. YO8: Bray 4A 58
Brackenhills YO26: Up P 4B 16
Bracken Rd. YO24: York 2H 37
Bradley Cres. YO23: Ruff 4D 24
Bradley Dr. YO24: York 1E 37
Bradley La. YO23: Ruff 4E 25
Braeside Gdns. YO24: York 4G 27
YO26: York 4G 27
Brailsford Cres. YO30: York 5A 18
Braithegayte YO19: Whel 4B 50
Bramble Dene YO24: York 2F 37
Bramble Gro. YO31: York 3E 19
Bramham Av. YO26: York 4C 26
Bramham Gro. YO26: York 4C 26
Bramham Rd. YO26: York 5C 26
Bramley Av. YO8: B'by 4F 57
Bramley Gth. YO31: York 1H 29
Brandon Gro. YO32: York 2C 20
Brandsby Gro. YO31: York 3E 19
Brandsdale Cres. YO10: Osb 4B 30
Bransholme Dr. YO30: York 3A 18
Brant La. LS24: Stut 6C 54
Branton Pl. YO26: York 4C 26
Bray Rd. YO10: York 1E 39
BRAYTON 6B 58
Brayton Junc. YO8: Bray 6D 58
Brayton La. YO8: Bray 6B 58
Breary Cl. YO24: York 6H 27
Brecks Cl. YO32: Wigg 3C 10
Brecksfield YO30: Ske 6E 9
Brecks La. YO30: Ske 6F 9
YO32: Hunt 1F 19
YO32: Stre 3B 6

A-Z York 61

Brend La.—Coggan Way

Brend La. YO10: H'tn 2B 40
Brentwood Cres. YO10: York 5A 30
Bretgate YO1: York 4G 3
Briar Av. YO26: York 3D 26
Briar Cliffe YO8: Bray 4B 58
Briar Dr. YO31: York 3F 19
Bridge Cl. YO32: Hax 4C 10
Bridge Ct. YO8: Sel 1E 59
Bridge Gth. YO10: H'tn 6H 29
Bridge La. YO30: York 1C 28
YO31: York 1C 28
Bridge Rd. YO23: Bish 6H 37
Bridges Ct. YO8: Sel 1E 59
Bridge St. YO1: York 4D 2 (3C 28)
YO26: Tad 3E 55
Bridle Wlk. YO8: Sel 3D 58
Bridle Way YO26: York 4C 26
Bridlington Rd. YO41: Stam B 4H 23
Briergate YO32: Hax 4C 10
Brigantium Roman Fort 2D 30
Briggs St. YO31: York 6C 18
Bright St. YO26: York 2H 27
Bright Wlk. YO8: Sel 1C 58
Brinkworth Ter.
YO10: York 5H 3 (4E 29)
Broad Acres YO32: Hax 4C 10
Broad Highway YO19: Whel 2A 50
Broadlands YO19: Whel 4C 50
Broad La. YO23: App R, Aca M 6D 44
YO23: York 5C 26
YO26: Neth P 3F 15
YO41: Low C 1H 33
Broad Oak La. YO32: Wigg 2B 10
Broadstone Way YO30: York 2G 17
Broadway YO10: York 1D 38
Broadway Gro. YO10: York 1E 39
Broadway W. YO10: York 1D 38
Brockfield Hall 3G 21
Brockfield La. YO19: W'hil 2H 21
Brockfield Pk. Dr. YO31: York 3E 19
Brockfield Rd. YO31: York 3E 19
Bromley St. YO26: York 2H 27
Brompton Rd. YO30: York 6A 18
Brooklands YO10: Osb 3B 30
Brook St. YO8: Sel 3C 58
YO31: York 1C 28
Broome Cl. YO32: Hunt 6F 11
Broome Rd. YO32: Hunt 6G 11
Broome Way YO32: Hunt 6G 11
Broom Rd. YO26: Tad 4C 54
Brougham Cl. YO30: York 5H 17
Broughton Way YO10: York 3H 29
Browney Cft. YO10: York 6F 3 (4D 28)
Brownlow St. YO31: York 1D 28
Brown Moor Rd. YO41: Stam B 5H 23
Brown's Paddock YO26: Stut 6C 54
Brunel Ct. YO26: York 2H 27
Brunswick Cl. YO32: Stre 2C 6
Brunswick Pl. YO1: York 3F 3 (3D 28)
Brunswick St. YO23: York 6B 28
Bryony Ct. YO8: Sel 5C 58
Buccaneer Ct. YO41: Elv 4C 42
Buckden Ho. *YO26: York* *3F 27*
(off Bouthwaite Dr.)
Buckingham Ct. YO1: York 5D 2
Buckingham St.
YO1: York 5D 2 (4C 28)
Buckingham Ter. *YO1: York* *5D 2*
(off Bishophill Senior)
Buckle Ct. YO8: Sel 1C 58
Bull Commercial Cen.
YO32: Stock F 2D 20
Buller St. YO8: Sel 1C 58
Bull La. YO10: York 3F 29
YO31: York 1F 29
Bungalow Rd. YO8: Sel 1E 59
Burdyke Av. YO30: York 5A 18
Burgess Wlk. YO24: York 1E 37
Burlands La. YO26: Up P 1A 26
Burlington Av. YO10: York 3F 29
Burn Est. YO32: Hunt 1E 19
Burnholme Av. YO31: York 1G 29
Burnholme Dr. YO31: York 1G 29
Burnholme Gro. YO31: York 2G 29
Burniston Gro. YO10: York 3G 29
Burniston Ho. *YO31: York* *1C 28*
(off Pilgrim St.)
Burnsall Dr. YO26: York 3G 27
Burns Ct. YO24: York 2D 36
Burrell's La. YO30: Ship 1A 8
Burrill Av. YO30: York 5B 18
Burrill Dr. YO32: Wigg 2A 10
Burton Av. YO30: York 6B 18
Burton Cft. YO30: York 1B 28
Burton Flds. Cl. YO41: Stam B 4H 23
Burton Flds. Rd. YO41: Stam B 4H 23
Burton Grn. YO30: York 5B 18
(not continuous)
Burton Stone La. YO30: York 1B 28
Burtree Av. YO30: Ske 6E 9
Butcher Ter. YO23: York 6C 28
Buttacre La. YO23: Ask R 5F 35
Buttercrambe Rd.
YO41: Stam B 4G 23
Buttermere Ct. YO8: Sel 1C 58
Buttermere Dr. YO30: York 4G 17
Butters Cl. YO32: Wigg 2B 10
Butt Hill YO32: Wigg 2B 10
Butts Cl. YO41: Stam B 5G 23
Byland Av. YO31: York 5E 19
Byron Dr. YO30: York 5H 17

C

Caedmon Cl. YO31: York 6G 19
Caesar Ct. YO23: York 6C 2 (4B 28)
Cairnborrow YO24: York 2D 36
Caithness Cl. YO30: York 2G 17
Calcaria Ct. YO24: York 1H 37
Calcaria Cres. YO26: Tad 4C 54
Calcaria Rd. YO26: Tad 4C 54
Caldbeck Cl. YO30: York 4A 18
Calder Av. YO26: Neth P 5D 16
Calder Ho. YO10: York 5G 3
Calf Cl. YO32: Hax 3D 10
Calvert Cl. YO32: Hax 4C 10
Cambrian Cl. YO32: Hunt 2F 19
Cambridge M. YO24: York 5A 2
Cambridge St.
YO24: York 5A 2 (4A 28)
Cameron Gro. YO23: York 6C 28
Cameron Walker Ct.
YO23: York *6C 28*
(off Bishopthorpe Rd.)
Campbell Av. YO24: York 5G 27
Campbell Ct. YO10: Osb 3H 29
Campleshon Rd. YO23: York 6B 28
Canal Rd. YO8: Sel 3E 59
Canal Vw. YO8: Sel 3E 59
Canham Gro. YO10: Osb 4B 30
Canons Ct. YO23: Bish 1B 46
Canterbury Cl. YO32: Wigg 1B 10
Carentan Cl. YO8: Sel 1C 58
Carey St. YO10: York 6D 28
Carleton St. YO26: York 2H 27
Carlisle St. YO26: York 2H 27
Carl St. YO23: York 5C 28
Carlton Av. YO10: York 4H 29
Carlton Cotts. YO32: Wigg 1B 10
Carlton Ho. YO24: York 6F 27
Carlton Rd. YO41: Sutt D 1H 51
Carlton Vw. YO8: Sel 3E 59
Carmelite St. YO1: York 3F 3 (3D 28)
Carmires Av. YO32: Hax 2E 11
Carnaby Ho. *YO31: York* *1D 28*
(off Jackson St.)
Carnot St. YO26: York 2H 27
Carnoustie Cl. YO26: York 3D 26
Caroline Cl. YO24: York 4H 27
Carrbank La. YO32: Stock F 6F 13
Carrfield YO24: York 1E 37
CARR HILL 3F 27
Carrick Gdns. YO24: York 4G 27
Carrington Av. YO26: York 2G 27
Carr La. YO8: Sel 6F 57
(not continuous)
YO19: Esc 3F 53
YO19: Ric 3B 56
YO19: Whel 5E 51
YO26: York 3F 27
Carrnock Ct. YO32: Hunt 4F 19
Carron Cres. YO24: York 2D 36
Carr's La. YO1: York 5D 2
Carrs Mdw. YO19: Esc 3G 53
Carr St. YO8: Sel 3G 59
Carter Av. YO31: York 2F 29
Castle Cl. YO32: Wigg 1A 10
Castlegate YO1: York 4E 3 (3C 28)
Castle Mus. 5F 3 (4D 28)
Castleton Ho. *YO31: York* *1C 28*
(off Garden St.)
Castle Wlk. *YO1: York* *4E 3*
(off Castlegate)
Catherine Ct.
YO10: York 4H 3 (4E 29)
Cat La. YO23: Bilb 6G 35
YO26: Hess 6F 15
Catterton La. YO26: Tad 1H 55
Cavendish Gro. YO10: Osb 4B 30
Caxton Av. YO26: York 1F 27
Cayley Cl. YO30: York 4H 17
Cecilia Pl.
YO24: York 5A 2 (4A 28)
Cedar Cres. YO8: Sel 3A 58
Cedar Dr. YO26: Tad 3C 54
Cedar Glade YO19: Dun 2H 31
Cedar Gro. YO31: York 6H 19
Cedarwood Cl. YO24: York 6D 26
Celtic Cl. YO26: York 2D 26
Cemetery Rd.
YO10: York 6G 3 (5D 28)
Centre La. YO26: Tad 3E 55
Centurion Pk. YO30: York 3B 18
Centurion Sq. YO1: York 4D 2
Centurion Way YO30: York 2B 18
Chaldon Cl. YO32: Stre 5H 5
Chalfonts YO24: York 6H 27
Chaloner's Cres. YO24: York 2F 37
Chaloner's Rd. YO24: York 1F 37
Chancery Ct. YO24: York 4E 27
Chancery Ho. *YO24: York* *4H 27*
(off Holgate Rd.)
Chancery Ri. *YO24: York* *4H 27*
(off Holgate Rd.)
Chantry Av. YO26: Up P 4B 16
Chantry Cl. YO24: York 1E 37
Chantry Gap YO26: Up P 4B 16
Chantry Gro. YO26: Up P 4B 16
Chantry La. YO23: Bish 5B 38
CHAPEL FIELDS 4D 26
Chapel Flds. Rd. YO26: York 4C 26
Chapel La. YO8: Bray 6C 58
YO19: Ric 2B 56
YO23: Ask B 4A 36
Chapel Row YO1: York 5G 3 (4D 28)
Chapel St. YO26: Tad 3D 54
Chapel Ter. YO24: York 4E 27
Chapel Wlk. YO19: Ric 3B 56
Chapman Cl. YO32: Stre 2C 6
Chapman Ho. *YO23: York* *5C 28*
(off Beway St.)
Chapmans Ct. YO24: York 3F 37
Chapter Ho. St.
YO1: York 2E 3 (2C 28)
Charles Ct. YO32: Stre 2B 6
Charles Moor YO31: York 6F 19
Charles St. YO8: Sel 1B 58
Charles Wesley Dr. YO8: Bray 6C 58
Charlotte St. YO10: York 4H 3 (3E 29)
Charlton St. YO23: York 5C 28
Charters, The YO8: B'by 3F 57
Chase Side Ct. YO24: York 1G 37
Chatsworth Av. YO32: Stre 2B 6
Chatsworth Dr. YO32: Hax 2F 11
Chatsworth Ter. YO26: York 3G 27
Chaucer La. YO32: Stre 2B 6
Chaucer St. YO10: York 4E 29
Chaumont Way YO32: Stock F 1E 21
Checker La. YO19: Ric 4B 56
Chelkar Way YO30: York 4H 17
Chelwood Wlk. YO26: York 3G 27
Cherry Gth. YO31: York 2H 29
Cherry Gro. YO26: Up P 4B 16
Cherry Hill Ho. *YO23: York* *6E 3*
(off Bishopgate St.)
Cherry Hill La. YO23: York 6E 3
Cherry La. YO24: York 1H 37
Cherry Orchard YO32: Hax 3D 10
Cherry Paddock YO32: Hax 3D 10
YO41: Stam B 2H 23
Cherry St. YO23: York 6E 3 (4C 28)
Cherry Tree Av. YO32: New E 1D 18
Cherry Tree Cl. YO8: Bray 6A 58
Cherry Tree Ct. YO8: B'by 5F 57
Cherry Tree Dr. YO23: Aca M 6G 45
Cherry Tree Wlk. YO8: B'by 5F 57
Cherrytree Wlk. YO26: Tad 4C 54
(not continuous)
Cherry Wood Cres. YO19: Ful 4E 39
Cheshire Av. YO32: Stre 6H 5
Cheshire Ct. YO30: York 3G 17
Chesney Flds. YO24: York 6F 27
Chessingham Gdns.
YO24: York 3G 37
Chessingham Pk. YO19: Dun 3A 32
Chestnut Av. YO31: York 1F 29
Chestnut Cotts. YO41: Gate H 2E 23
Chestnut Ct. YO32: Hunt 6F 11
Chestnut Farm Cvn. Pk.
YO23: Aca M 3A 46
Chestnut Gro. YO26: York 3E 27
YO32: New E 2E 19
Chestnuts, The YO32: Wigg 3C 10
Chestnut Ter. *YO19: Ric* *3A 56*
(off Back La.)
Cheviot Cl. YO32: Hunt 2F 19
Chiltern Way YO32: Hunt 6F 11
Chilvers Ct. YO8: Bray 6B 58
Chimes, The YO8: Sel 1D 58
Chipstead Wlk. YO32: Stre 4H 5
Chrennicar La. YO23: Bilb 6E 35
Chudleigh Rd. YO26: York 2H 27
Church Balk YO19: Dun 1H 31
Church Cl. YO19: Ric 3A 56
YO19: Whel 5C 50
YO23: Ask B 3A 36
Church Cres. YO26: Stut 6C 54
Church Farm Cl. YO23: Ruff 4D 24
CHURCH FIELD 2C 10
Churchfield Dr. YO32: Wigg 2C 10
Church Grn. YO41: Elv 5F 43
Church Hill YO8: Sel 2E 59
Church La. YO1: York 4E 3 (3C 28)
YO8: B'by 5F 57
YO8: Sel 2E 59
YO19: Dun 1H 31
YO19: Whel 5C 50
YO23: Bish 5A 38
YO26: Moor M 1A 14
YO26: Neth P 3C 16
YO26: Stut 6C 54
YO30: Ske 6D 8
YO32: Hunt 6F 11
YO32: Stre 3H 5
YO32: Wigg 2C 10
YO41: Elv 6G 43
YO41: Stam B 5G 23
Church M. YO8: B'by 4F 57
YO26: York 4E 27
Church Ri. YO19: Holt 4B 22
Church Rd. YO10: Osb 3B 30
YO41: Stam B 5G 23
Church St. YO1: York 3E 3 (3C 28)
YO19: Dun 1H 31
YO19: Ric 3A 56
YO23: Cop 1D 44
Cinder La. YO26: Neth P 2H 15
YO26: Up P 6C 16
YO26: York 2A 2 (2A 28)
(Kensington Ho.)
YO26: York 4A 2 (3A 28)
(Railway Ter.)
YO26: York 2H 27
(St Barnabas Cl.)
YO31: York 1E 29
Cinder M. YO26: York 2A 28
City Art Gallery 1D 2 (2C 28)
City Ho. YO10: York 6G 3
City Mills YO1: York 5E 3 (4C 28)
City Screen Cinema 3D 2 (3C 28)
Claremont Ter.
YO31: York 1D 2 (1C 28)
Clarence St. YO31: York 1D 2 (1C 28)
Clarendon Ct. YO31: York 6C 18
Clarks Ter. *YO31: York* *1F 29*
(off Dale's La.)
Claygate YO31: York 1H 29
Clay Pl. YO24: York 6F 27
CLEMENTHORPE 5C 28
Clementhorpe
YO23: York 6E 3 (4C 28)
Clement St. YO23: York 6D 2 (4C 28)
Cleveland Gdns. YO32: Stock F 6F 13
Cleveland St. YO24: York 3A 28
Cleveland Ter. YO32: Hunt 1F 19
Cleveland Way YO32: Hunt 2F 19
Cliffe Rd. YO8: Osg 5H 57
Clifford Ho. YO1: York 5E 3
Clifford's Tower 4E 3 (3C 28)
Clifford St. YO1: York 4E 3 (3C 28)
CLIFTON 6A 18
Clifton Dale YO30: York 1A 28
Clifton Ga. Bus. Pk.
YO32: Wigg 6B 10
Clifton Grn. YO30: York 1A 28
CLIFTON MOOR 2A 18
Clifton Moor Bus. Village
YO30: York 3A 18
Clifton Moor Cen. YO30: York 2G 17
(not continuous)
Clifton Moor Ga. YO30: York 2H 17
Clifton Moor Ind. Est.
YO30: York 2A 18
Clifton Pk. Av. YO30: York 5G 17
CLIFTON PARK CAPIO NHS
TREATMENT CENTRE 5G 17
Clifton Pl. YO30: York 6A 18
Clifton Rd. YO30: York 6A 18
Clive Gro. YO24: York 5H 27
Cloisters Wlk.
YO31: York 2F 3 (2D 28)
Cloither Ct. *YO23: Cop* *6E 37*
(off Learmans Way)
Close, The YO23: Aca M 6G 45
YO30: York 5H 17
Cloverley Cl. YO41: Stam B 2H 23
Cobble Ct. M.
YO24: York 6B 2 (4B 28)
Cobham Way YO30: York 2G 17
Cochrane St. YO8: Sel 4E 59
Cockret Cl. YO8: Sel 1C 58
Cockret Ct. *YO8: Sel* *1C 58*
(off Cockret Rd.)
Cockret Rd. YO8: Sel 1C 58
Coda Av. YO23: Bish 6B 38
Coeside YO24: York 2D 36
Coffee Yd. YO1: York 2E 3
Coggan Cl. YO23: York 5B 28
Coggan Way YO23: Bish 5H 37

Elston Pl.—Greenside

Elston Pl. YO8: Sel ... 1D 58
ELVINGTON ... 5G 43
Elvington Brickyard Windpump ... 1C 50
Elvington Ind. Est. YO41: Elv ... 4D 42
Elvington La.
YO19: Dun, Grim ... 4E 31
YO41: Elv ... 4E 31
Elvington Pk. YO41: Elv ... 4D 42
Elvington Ter.
YO10: York ... 4H 3 (3E 29)
Elwick Gro. YO10: York ... 3A 30
Embleton Dr. YO30: York ... 4H 17
Emerald St. YO31: York ... 1D 28
Emily M. YO10: York ... 3E 29
Emmerson St.
YO31: York ... 1H 3 (2E 29)
Emperors Wharf
YO1: York ... 5E 3 (4C 28)
Enclosure Gdns. YO10: H'tn ... 6H 29
Endfields Rd. YO10: York ... 1E 39
Enfield Cres. YO24: York ... 4H 27
Engelhart Cl. YO8: Bray ... 5B 58
Ennerdale Av. YO31: York ... 2H 29
ESCRICK ... 3F 53
Escrick Ct. YO19: Esc ... 3G 53
Escrick Pk. Gdns. YO19: Esc ... 4G 53
Escrick Rd. YO19: Still ... 6A 52
Escrick St. YO10: York ... 6G 3 (4D 28)
Escrick Ter. YO10: York ... 6G 3
Eskdale Av. YO10: Osb ... 4A 30
Esk Dr. YO26: Neth P ... 5D 16
Esplanade, The
YO30: York ... 1A 2 (1H 27)
Esplanade Ct. YO30: York ... 2B 2
Etive Pl. YO24: York ... 2D 36
Eton Dr. YO32: Wigg ... 1B 10
Etty Av. YO10: York ... 3G 29
Etty Cl. YO41: Stam B ... 5H 23
Eva Av. YO30: York ... 3F 17
Evelyn Cres. YO30: York ... 6B 18
Evergreen Way YO8: Bray ... 5A 58
Exhibition Sq.
YO1: York ... 2D 2 (2C 28)
Eyre Cl. YO8: Bray ... 5B 58

F

Faber Cl. YO23: Cop ... 6D 36
Faber St. YO31: York ... 1H 3 (2E 29)
Fairfax YO41: Stam B ... 5G 23
Fairfax Av. YO8: Sel ... 3C 58
Fairfax Ct. YO24: York ... 4F 27
Fairfax Cft. YO23: Cop ... 1D 44
Fairfax House ... 4E 3
Fairfax St. YO1: York ... 5D 2 (4C 28)
Fairfield Ct. YO24: York ... 6F 27
Fairfield Rd. YO26: Tad ... 3D 54
Fairfields Dr. YO30: Ske ... 6D 8
Fairfield Way YO26: Tad ... 3D 54
Fairway YO8: Sel ... 3B 58
YO30: York ... 5A 18
Fairway, The YO26: Tad ... 5D 54
Fairway Dr. YO26: Up P ... 4B 16
Falcon Cl. YO32: Hax ... 2E 11
Falconer St. YO24: York ... 4H 27
Falkland St. YO1: York ... 5D 2 (4C 28)
Falsgrave Cres. YO30: York ... 6B 18
Fanny La. YO26: Stut ... 6C 54
Farfield YO26: York ... 1E 27
Farfield La. YO19: Holt ... 5G 21
Farmers Way YO23: Cop ... 6D 36
Farmlands Rd. YO24: York ... 1F 37
Farmstead Ri. YO32: Hax ... 4D 10
Farm Way YO8: Sel ... 1C 58
Farndale Av. YO10: Osb ... 3B 30
Farndale Cl. YO32: Hax ... 1E 11
Farndale St. YO10: York ... 5D 28
Farrar St. YO10: York ... 6H 3 (4E 29)
Farriers Chase YO32: Stre ... 6H 5
Farriers Cft. YO23: Cop ... 6D 36
Fawcett St. YO10: York ... 6G 3 (4D 28)
Fawkes Dr. YO26: York ... 3E 27
Feasegate YO1: York ... 3E 3 (3C 28)
Fellbrook Av. YO26: York ... 3D 26
Fenwick's La. YO10: Ful ... 2D 38
Fenwick St. YO23: York ... 5C 28
Ferguson Way YO32: Hunt ... 4F 19
Fern Cl. YO32: Hunt ... 1G 19
Fern Ct. YO19: Ric ... 2B 56
Ferndale Rd. YO8: Sel ... 3D 58
Fernlea Cl. YO8: Sel ... 3E 59
Fern St. YO31: York ... 1F 3 (1D 28)
Fernway YO10: York ... 4A 30
Ferry Farm Cl. YO19: Nab ... 3B 46
Ferry La. YO23: Bish ... 5B 38
Ferrymans Wlk. YO26: Neth P ... 2B 16
Festival Flats YO10: York ... 6F 3
Fetter La. YO1: York ... 4D 2 (3C 28)
Feversham Cres. YO31: York ... 6C 18
Feversham Ga. *YO31: York ... 6C 18*
(off Feversham Cres.)
Feversham Ho. YO31: York ... 2F 3
Fewster Way YO10: York ... 6F 3 (4D 28)
Fewston Dr. YO30: York ... 4H 17
Field Ct. YO31: York ... 1G 29
Field Dr. YO26: Tad ... 1G 55
Field La. YO10: H'tn, York ... 6H 29
Fieldside Pl. YO10: York ... 3F 29
Field Vw. YO30: York ... 6C 18
Fifth Av. YO31: York ... 1H 3 (2E 29)
Filey Ter. YO30: York ... 6C 18
Finkle St. YO1: York ... 3E 3
YO8: Sel ... 2D 58
Finsbury Av. YO23: York ... 6C 28
Finsbury St. YO23: York ... 6C 28
Firbank Cl. YO32: Stre ... 4H 5
Fir Heath Cl. YO24: York ... 6E 27
Firs Gth. La. YO41: Stam B ... 4G 23
First Av. YO31: York ... 1F 29
Firth M. YO8: Sel ... 1D 58
Firtree Cl. YO24: York ... 4G 27
YO32: Ear ... 4F 11
Firtree Cres. YO26: Tad ... 5C 54
Firwood Whin YO31: York ... 3F 19
Fishergate YO10: York ... 5F 3 (4D 28)
Fishergate Ho.
YO10: York ... 6F 3 (5D 28)
Fitzroy Ter. YO10: York ... 6H 3 (4E 29)
Flavian Gro. YO30: York ... 5H 17
Flaxley Ct. YO8: Sel ... 1B 58
Flaxley Rd. YO8: Sel ... 1A 58
Flaxman Av. YO10: York ... 3G 29
Flaxman Cft. YO23: Cop ... 6D 36
Flaxton Rd. YO32: Stre ... 4B 6
Fleming Av. YO31: York ... 1H 3 (2E 29)
Fletcher Ct. YO32: Wigg ... 2C 10
Fletchers Cotts. YO8: Sel ... 6F 57
Fletcher's Cft. YO23: Cop ... 6E 37
Florence Gro. YO30: York ... 3F 17
Fold, The YO26: Hess ... 6C 14
Fold Wlk. YO32: Stre ... 2B 6
Folks Cl. YO32: Hax ... 2E 11
Fordlands Cres. YO19: Ful ... 3E 39
Fordlands Rd. YO19: Ful ... 3E 39
Forest Cl. YO32: Wigg ... 2C 10
Forest Ct. YO32: Stre ... 4H 5
Foresters Wlk. YO24: York ... 6D 26
YO41: Stam B ... 3H 23
Forestgate YO32: Hax ... 4C 10
Forest Gro. YO31: York ... 1F 29
Forest La. YO19: Crock H, Ful ... 5G 39
YO32: Stre ... 2G 5
Forest Way YO31: York ... 1F 29
Forge Cl. YO19: Whel ... 5C 50
YO32: Hunt ... 3G 19
Forge La. YO19: Dei ... 6H 47
Forth St. YO26: York ... 1H 27
Foss Bank YO31: York ... 1G 3 (2D 28)
Foss Ct. YO31: York ... 4E 19
Foss Fld. La. YO23: Aca M ... 4F 45
Fossgate YO1: York ... 3F 3 (3D 28)
FOSS ISLANDS ... 3H 3 (3E 29)
Foss Islands Rd.
YO31: York ... 2G 3 (2D 28)
Fossland Vw. YO32: Stre ... 3H 5
Foss Wlk. YO26: Neth P ... 5D 16
Fossway YO31: York ... 6D 18
YO41: Stam B ... 6G 23
Fostergate YO8: Sel ... 3E 59
Foston Gro. YO31: York ... 5F 19
Fountains Cl. YO19: Ric ... 3B 56
Fountayne Ho. *YO10: York ... 4F 29*
(off Lawrence Sq.)
Fountayne St. YO31: York ... 6C 18
Fourth Av. YO31: York ... 2E 29
Fox Covert YO31: York ... 3F 19
Foxcroft YO32: Hax ... 5C 10
Fox Gth. YO26: Neth P ... 2C 16
Fox Glade YO41: Stam B ... 2H 23
Foxhill La. YO8: Bray, Sel ... 5B 58
Foxoak Pk. YO19: Dun ... 3A 32
Foxthorn Paddock
YO10: York ... 4B 30
Foxton YO24: York ... 1E 37
Foxwood La. YO24: York ... 6D 26
France Ind. Complex
YO8: Sel ... 2E 59
Frances St. YO10: York ... 6D 28
Franklin's Yd. *YO1: York ... 4F 3*
(off Fossgate)
Frazer Ct. YO30: York ... 5G 17
Frederic St. YO30: York ... 2B 2 (2B 28)
Friargate YO1: York ... 4E 3 (3C 28)
Friargate Theatre ... 4E 3
Friars Ter. YO1: York ... 5E 3
Friar's Wlk. YO31: York ... 5E 19
Friendship Ct. YO8: Sel ... 1D 58
Front St. YO19: Nab ... 3B 46
YO24: York ... 4E 27
Fryors Cl. YO19: Mur ... 2E 31
FULFORD ... 2E 39
Fulford Chase YO10: York ... 1D 38
Fulford Cross YO10: York ... 6D 28
Fulfordgate YO10: York ... 2E 39
Fulford Ind. Est. YO10: York ... 6D 28
Fulford M. YO10: Ful ... 3E 39
Fulford Pk. YO10: Ful ... 2D 38
Fulford Rd. YO10: York ... 5D 28
Furlong Rd. YO41: Stam B ... 5H 23
Furness Dr. YO30: York ... 4G 17
Furnwood YO32: Hax ... 4D 10
Fylingdale Av. YO30: York ... 5G 17

G

Gable Pk. YO23: Ruff ... 4D 24
Gainsborough Cl. YO32: Stre ... 2B 6
Gale Farm Ct. YO24: York ... 4E 27
Gale La. YO24: York ... 4E 27
Galligap La. YO10: Osb ... 2A 30
Gallops, The YO24: York ... 1D 36
GALLOWS HILL ... 2E 55
Galmanhoe La.
YO30: York ... 1C 2 (2B 28)
Galtres Av. YO31: York ... 6H 19
Galtres Gro. YO30: York ... 6H 17
Galtres Rd. YO31: York ... 6H 19
Ganton Pl. YO24: York ... 2G 37
Gant Wlk. *YO8: Sel ... 2E 59*
(off Church La.)
Garbett Way YO23: Bish ... 6B 38
Garburn Gro. YO30: York ... 4G 17
Garbutt Gro. YO26: York ... 2F 27
Garden Ct. YO8: Sel ... 1C 58
YO26: York ... 2E 27
Gardeners Cl. YO23: Cop ... 6D 36
Garden Flats La. YO19: Dun ... 1H 31
Garden Pl. YO1: York ... 3F 3 (3D 28)
Garden St. YO31: York ... 1F 3 (1C 28)
Garden Village, The YO32: Ear ... 3G 11
Garden Way YO26: York ... 2E 27
Garfield Ter. YO26: York ... 2H 27
Gargrave Ho. *YO26: York ... 3G 27*
(off Burnsall Dr.)
Garlands, The YO30: York ... 5A 18
Garland St. YO26: York ... 3G 27
Garnet La. YO26: Tad ... 6A 54
Garnet Ter. YO26: Tad ... 5B 54
YO26: York ... 2G 27
Garrick Cl. YO8: Bray ... 6C 58
Garrowby Vw. YO41: Stam B ... 4H 23
Garrowby Way YO10: H'tn ... 1H 39
Garrow Hill YO10: York ... 5F 29
Garrow Hill Av. YO10: York ... 4G 29
Garth Ct. YO32: Hunt ... 1G 19
Garth End YO32: Hunt ... 1F 19
Garth Rd. YO32: Hunt ... 1F 19
Garths End YO10: York ... 1E 39
YO32: Hax ... 2F 11
Garth Ter. YO30: York ... 6B 18
Garth Way YO32: New E ... 2D 18
Gascoigne Wlk. YO23: York ... 6D 2
GATE HELMSLEY ... 2E 23
Gateland Cl. YO32: Hax ... 4C 10
Gatesby Ho. *YO24: York ... 5A 2*
(off Cambridge St.)
Gay Mdws. YO32: Stock F ... 1F 21
Geldof Rd. YO32: Hunt ... 4F 19
George Cayley Dr. YO30: York ... 2A 18
George Ct. YO31: York ... 1G 3 (1D 28)
George Hudson St.
YO1: York ... 4D 2 (3C 28)
George St. YO1: York ... 5F 3 (4D 28)
YO8: Sel ... 1E 59
George Ter. YO8: B'by ... 5F 57
Gerard Av. YO31: York ... 2G 29
Germain Rd. YO8: Sel ... 3F 59
Germany La. YO10: Ful ... 3E 39
YO19: Ful ... 3E 39
Ghost Trail of York, The ... 2D 2
Giles Av. YO31: York ... 2G 29
Gillamoor Av. YO31: York ... 2H 29
Gillingwood Rd. YO30: York ... 2H 17
Gillygate YO31: York ... 1D 2 (2C 28)
Girvan Cl. YO24: York ... 2D 36
Gisburn Ho. *YO26: York ... 3G 27*
(off Burnsall Dr.)
Givendale Gro. YO10: Osb ... 3A 30
Glade, The YO19: Esc ... 3G 53
YO31: York ... 6H 19
Gladstone St. YO24: York ... 4F 27
YO31: York ... 1D 28
Glaisby Ct. YO31: York ... 1G 29
Glaisdale YO24: York ... 2F 37
Glaisdale Rd. YO26: Up P ... 1B 26
Glebe, The YO19: Dun ... 1H 31
Glebe Av. YO26: York ... 2F 27
Glebe Cl. YO32: Stre ... 4A 6
Glebe Gth. YO8: B'by ... 4F 57
Glebe Way YO32: Hax ... 2C 10
Glen Av. YO31: York ... 1H 3 (2E 29)
Glen Cl. YO10: Ful ... 3E 39
Glencoe St. YO30: York ... 6B 18
Glen Lodge YO31: York ... 2E 29
Glenridding YO24: York ... 2F 37
Glen Rd. YO31: York ... 1H 3 (2E 29)
Glenside Flats YO31: York ... 2E 29
Godwinsway YO41: Stam B ... 5H 23
Golf Links Av. YO26: Tad ... 4C 54
Golf Links Ct. YO26: Tad ... 4D 54
Golf Links Cres. YO26: Tad ... 4C 54
Goodramgate YO1: York ... 2E 3 (2C 28)
Goodricke Way YO10: H'tn ... 6G 29
Goodwood Gro. YO24: York ... 6H 27
Gordon St. YO10: York ... 6H 3 (4E 29)
Gormire Av. YO31: York ... 3E 19
Gorse Cl. YO8: Sel ... 5D 58
Gorse Hill YO19: Dun ... 1A 32
Gorse Paddock YO31: York ... 3F 19
Gouthwaith Cl. YO30: York ... 3H 17
Government Ho. Rd.
YO30: York ... 1A 28
Gower Rd. YO24: York ... 1G 37
Gowland Ct. YO1: York ... 1E 3
Gowthorpe YO8: Sel ... 2C 58
Grampian Cl. YO32: Hunt ... 6F 11
Granary Ct. YO1: York ... 2F 3 (2D 28)
Grand Opera House ... 4E 3
Grange Av. YO26: Tad ... 2F 55
Grange Cl. YO30: Ske ... 6D 8
Grange Cres. YO26: Tad ... 2E 55
Grange Farm Cl. YO8: B'by ... 3F 57
Grange Gth. YO10: York ... 5D 28
Grange Ho. *YO30: York ... 1B 28*
(off Nth. Grange Ct.)
Grange La. YO23: York ... 5H 25
YO26: York ... 5H 25
Granger Av. YO26: York ... 3E 27
Grange Rd. YO26: Tad ... 2F 55
Grange St. YO10: York ... 5D 28
Grantham Dr. YO26: York ... 4G 27
Grants Av. YO10: York ... 1E 39
Granville Ter.
YO10: York ... 5H 3 (4E 29)
Grape La. YO1: York ... 2E 3 (2C 28)
Grasmere Dr. YO10: York ... 3H 29
Grasmere Gro. YO30: York ... 4H 17
Grassholme YO24: York ... 2E 37
Gray's Ct. YO1: York ... 1E 3
Grayshon Dr. YO26: York ... 2D 26
Gray St. YO23: York ... 6C 2 (4B 28)
Great Nth. Way YO26: Neth P ... 4D 16
Green, The YO19: Dun ... 2A 32
YO26: Up P ... 4B 16
YO26: York ... 4E 27
YO30: Ske ... 5D 8
YO41: Elv ... 5F 43
Greenacres YO32: Hunt ... 1F 19
Greenacres Cl. YO8: Bray ... 5A 58
Greenacres Cres. YO8: Bray ... 5A 58
Greenacres Dr. YO8: Bray ... 5A 58
Greenacres Gro. YO8: Bray ... 5A 58
Greenacres Mobile Home Pk.
YO8: Sel ... 1A 58
Green Balk YO23: Cop ... 2B 44
Green Bank Rd. *YO41: Stam B ... 5G 23*
(off Moor Rd.)
Greencliffe Dr. YO30: York ... 1A 28
Green Cl. YO30: York ... 5A 18
Greencroft Ct. YO19: Dun ... 2A 32
Greencroft La. YO19: Dun ... 2A 32
Green Dike YO32: Wigg ... 2B 10
Green Dykes La. YO10: York ... 4F 29
Greenfield Dr. YO8: Bray ... 5A 58
Greenfield Pk. Dr. YO31: York ... 6G 19
Greenfields YO31: York ... 6D 18
Greengales Ct. YO19: Whel ... 4C 50
Greengales La. YO19: Whel ... 4C 50
Green La. YO8: Sel ... 3B 58
YO10: H'tn ... 6B 30
YO19: Ric ... 5C 56
YO23: Ruff ... 2B 24
YO23: York ... 4H 37
YO24: York ... 4F 27
(Front St.)
YO24: York ... 4H 37
(Sim Balk La.)
YO26: Stut ... 6C 54
YO30: York ... 4H 17
YO32: Stre ... 2C 6
YO32: Wigg ... 1A 10
Green La. Trad. Est.
YO30: York ... 4A 18
Green Mdws. YO31: York ... 5G 19
Greensborough Av. YO26: York ... 2D 26
Greenshaw Dr.
YO32: Hax, Wigg ... 2B 10
Greenside YO19: Dun ... 2A 32

Greenside Cl.—Ings Vw.

Greenside Cl. YO19: Dun 2A **32**
Greenside Wlk. YO19: Dun 2A **32**
Green Sward YO31: York 5G **19**
Green Way YO32: Hunt 1F **19**
Greenway, The YO32: Hax 4C **10**
Greenwich Cl. YO30: York 2G **17**
Greenwood Gro. YO24: York 1E **37**
Gregory Cl. YO30: Ske 6E **9**
Gresley Ct. YO26: York 3D **26**
Greystoke Rd. YO30: York 4G **17**
Greystone Ct. YO32: Hax 5D **10**
GRIMSTON 3E **31**
GRIMSTON BAR 3D **30**
Grimwith Gth. YO30: York 3H **17**
Grosvenor Ho. *YO30: York 1B 28*
(off Grosvenor Ter.)
Grosvenor Pk. YO30: York 1B **28**
Grosvenor Rd. YO30: York 1B **28**
Grosvenor Ter.
YO30: York 1C **2** (1B **28**)
Grove, The YO24: York 3G **37**
Grove Gdns. YO26: Up P 4B **16**
Grove Pk. YO8: B'by 4F **57**
GROVES, THE 6D **18**
Groves Ct. YO31: York 1F **3**
Groves La. YO31: York 1F **3**
(not continuous)
Grove Ter. YO24: York 4E **27**
Grove Ter. La. YO31: York 1D **28**
Grove Vw. YO30: York 1A **28**
Guardian Ct. YO30: York 6A **18**
Guildhall
York 3D **2** (3C **28**)

H

Hackness Rd. YO26: Up P 1B **26**
Haddon Cl. YO24: York 5E **27**
Hadrian Av. YO10: York 4H **29**
Hagg La. LS24: Col 3A **44**
YO19: Dun 3B **32**
Haggwood Wlk. YO19: Whel 2A **50**
Haig St. YO8: Sel 1C **58**
Haley's Ter. YO31: York 5D **18**
Halfpenny Cl. YO19: Esc 3G **53**
Halifax Ct. YO30: York 4A **18**
Halifax Way YO41: Elv 4C **42**
Halladale Cl. YO24: York 2D **36**
Hallard Way YO32: Stre 4A **6**
Hall Cl. YO19: Whel 5C **50**
Hallcroft La. YO23: Cop 6C **36**
Hall Farm Cl. YO19: Ric 3A **56**
Hallfield Rd. YO31: York . . .1H **3** (2E **29**)
Hall Gth. YO8: Osg 5H **57**
Hallgarth Cl. YO26: Neth P 3B **16**
HALL MOOR 1D **8**
Hall Pk. YO8: B'by 4F **57**
YO10: H'tn 6H **29**
Hall Ri. YO32: Hax 2E **11**
Hambleton Av YO10: Osb 3A **30**
Hambleton Ter. YO31: York 6C **18**
Hambleton Vw. YO32: Wigg 1B **10**
Hambleton Way YO32: Hunt 2F **19**
Hamilton Dr. YO24: York 5G **27**
Hamilton Dr. E. YO24: York 5H **27**
Hamilton Dr. W. YO24: York 5F **27**
Hamilton Way YO24: York 5G **27**
Hammerton Cl. YO26: York 4D **26**
Hampden St. YO1: York . . .5D **2** (4C **28**)
Handley Cl. YO30: York 3A **18**
Hannam La. YO23: Ruff 4B **24**
Hanover Ct. YO32: Hax 2D **10**
Hanover St. E. YO26: York 2H **27**
Hanover St. W. YO26: York 2H **27**
Hansom Pl. YO31: York 6C **18**
Harcourt Cl. YO19: Whel 5B **50**
YO23: Bish 6A **38**
Harcourt St. YO31: York . . .1H **3** (2E **29**)
Harden Cl. YO30: York 3H **17**
Hardisty Cloisters *YO26: York 2A 28*
(off Hardisty M.)
Hardisty M. YO26: York 2H **27**
Hardrada Way YO41: Stam B 6G **23**
Hardy St. YO8: Sel 3F **59**
Harewood Cl. YO30: York 3F **17**
YO32: Wigg 1B **10**
Harewood Way YO10: H'tn 5G **29**
Harington Av. YO10: York 3F **29**
Harlequin Hgts. *YO8: Sel 1D 58*
(off Long Trods)
Harlow Cl. YO24: York 5H **27**
Harlow Ct. YO32: Stre 5H **5**
Harlow Rd. YO24: York 5H **27**
Harold Ct. YO24: York 4F **27**
Harold Hick Ct. YO26: Tad 2F **55**
Harold St. YO8: Sel 3G **59**
Harolds Way YO41: Stam B 6G **23**
Harper St. YO8: Sel 2D **58**
Harrier Ct. YO41: Elv 4C **42**
Harrisons Cl. YO41: Stam B 5G **23**
Harrison St. YO31: York 1F **29**
Harrow Glade YO30: York 4A **18**
Hartoft St. YO10: York 5D **28**
Harvest Cl. YO32: Stre 4A **6**
Harwood Rd. YO26: Up P 1B **26**
Hassacarr La. YO19: Dun 3A **32**
Hastings Cl. YO30: York 4A **18**
Hatfield Cl. YO30: York 2G **17**
Hatfield Wlk. YO24: York 1E **37**
Hatters Cl. YO23: Cop 6D **36**
Haughton Rd. YO30: York 6C **18**
Hauling La. YO23: Aca M 4H **45**
Haven, The YO8: Sel 2E **59**
Haverah Ct. YO30: York 4H **17**
Hawdon Av. YO8: Sel 2E **59**
Hawkshead Cl. YO24: York 1D **36**
Hawthorn Av. YO26: Tad 5C **54**
YO32: Hax 2D **10**
Hawthorn Cl. YO26: Tad 5D **54**
YO32: New E 2D **18**
Hawthorn Cft. YO26: Tad 5C **54**
Hawthorn Dr. YO8: B'by 4F **57**
Hawthorne Cl. YO26: Neth P 3B **16**
Hawthorne M. YO32: Stre 3A **6**
Hawthorn Gro.
YO31: York 1H **3** (2E **29**)
Hawthorn Pl. YO32: New E 1E **19**
Hawthorns YO19: Ric 3A **56**
Hawthorn Spinney YO31: York 2E **19**
Hawthorn St.
YO31: York 1H **3** (2E **29**)
Hawthorn Ter. YO32: New E 2D **18**
Hawthorn Ter. Central
YO32: New E 2D **18**
Hawthorn Ter. Nth.
YO32: New E 1D **18**
Hawthorn Ter. Sth.
YO32: New E 2D **18**
HAXBY .3D **10**
Haxby Moor Rd. YO32: Hax, Stre . . .4E **5**
Haxby Rd. YO31: York 1C **28**
YO32: Hax, New E 5D **10**
Hayforth Cl. YO30: York 3A **18**
Hazel Bush La. YO32: Stock F 3G **13**
Hazel Cl. YO32: New E 3D **18**
Hazel Ct. YO10: York 3H **3** (3E **29**)
Hazel Gth. YO31: York 6H **19**
Hazelmere Ct. YO32: Hunt 2E **19**
Hazelnut Gro. YO30: York 3B **18**
Hazelwood Av. YO10: Osb 3B **30**
Headland Cl. YO32: Hax 2C **10**
Headland Cl. YO32: Hax 3D **10**
Headley Cl. YO30: York 4B **18**
Healey Gro. YO31: York 5F **19**
Heath Cl. YO24: York 5H **27**
Heath Cft. YO10: York 2F **39**
Heather Bank YO10: Osb 3A **30**
YO41: Stam B 2H **23**
Heather Cl. YO8: Sel 4D **58**
YO32: Hunt 1G **19**
Heather Cft. YO31: York 3E **19**
Heatherdene YO26: Tad 2E **55**
Heather Way YO26: Tad 2E **55**
Heathfield Rd. YO10: York 4G **29**
Heath Moor Dr. YO10: York 1F **39**
Heath Ride YO32: Stre 2B **6**
Hebdon Ct. YO26: York 3F **27**
Hebdon Ri. YO26: York 3F **27**
Height Lands La. YO23: Ruff 4F **25**
Helmsdale YO24: York 2D **36**
Helmsley Gro. YO32: Wigg 2A **10**
Helmsley Ho. *YO10: York 4F 29*
(off Lawrence Sq.)
YO31: York 1D 28
(off Penley's Gro. St.)
Hemlock Av. YO31: York 4E **19**
Hempbridge Cl. YO8: Sel 2B **58**
Hempbridge Rd. YO8: Sel 1B **58**
Hempland Av. YO31: York 1F **29**
Hempland Dr. YO31: York 6G **19**
Hempland La. YO31: York 1G **29**
Hendon Gth. YO30: York 4A **18**
Henwick Hall La. YO8: Bray 6D **58**
Herbert St. YO10: York 4E **29**
Herberts Way YO31: York 6F **19**
Herdsman Dr. YO23: Cop 6E **37**
Herdsman Rd. YO24: York 1F **37**
Herdwick Cl. YO30: York 4B **18**
Heritage Ho. YO26: York 3G **27**
Herman Wlk. YO24: York 1E **37**
Heron Av. YO24: York 1E **37**
Heron Ho. YO10: York 5H **3**
Heron Ri. YO32: Hunt 6F **11**
Hesketh Bank YO10: York 4B **30**
Heslin Cl. YO32: Hax 3C **10**
HESLINGTON 6H **29**
Heslington Ct. YO10: H'tn 6H **29**
Heslington Cft. YO10: York 2F **39**
Heslington La. YO10: York 2E **39**
Heslington Rd.
YO10: York 6H **3** (4E **29**)
HESSAY 6C **14**
Hessay Ind. Est. YO26: Hess 5C **14**
Hessay Pl. YO26: York 4C **26**
Hetherton St. YO30: York . . .2B **2** (2B **28**)
Hewley Av. YO10: York 3F **29**
HEWORTH 6H **19**
Heworth YO31: York 1F **29**
Heworth Ct. YO31: York 1E **29**
Heworth Grn.
YO31: York 1G **3** (1D **28**)
Heworth Hall Dr. YO31: York 1F **29**
Heworth M. YO31: York 1H **3** (1E **29**)
Heworth Pl. YO31: York 1F **29**
Heworth Rd. YO31: York 1F **29**
Hickleton Ct. YO10: H'tn 1H **39**
High Catton Rd. YO41: Stam B . . .5G **23**
Highcliffe Ct. YO30: York 1A **28**
Highfield YO10: Osb 3B **30**
Highfield Ct. YO8: Bray 6C **58**
Highfield Cres. YO8: B'by 5F **57**
Highfield Vw. YO8: B'by 5F **57**
High Gth. YO32: Ear 4F **11**
Highgrove Cl. YO30: York 2G **17**
Highlands Av. YO32: Stre 4A **6**
High Mdw. YO8: Sel 1C **58**
Highmoor Cl. YO24: York 1F **37**
Highmoor Rd. YO24: York 1F **37**
High Newbiggin St.
YO31: York 1F **3** (2D **28**)
High Oaks YO31: York 6H **19**
High Ousegate
YO1: York 4E **3** (3C **28**)
High Petergate
YO1: York 2D **2** (2C **28**)
High St. YO26: Tad 3E **55**
Highthorn Rd. YO31: York 3E **19**
Hilbeck Gro. YO31: York 1H **29**
Hilbra Av. YO32: Hax 5D **10**
Hilda St. YO8: Sel 2D **58**
YO10: York 5H **3** (4E **29**)
Hillary Gth. YO26: York 3G **27**
Hillcrest YO19: Holt 4A **22**
YO26: Tad 4C **54**
Hillcrest Av. YO26: Neth P 3C **16**
Hillcrest Ct. YO26: Tad 4C **54**
Hillcrest Gdns. YO24: York 6H **27**
Hillgarth Ct. YO41: Elv 5F **43**
Hillsborough Ter. YO30: York 6C **18**
Hill St. YO24: York 4G **27**
Hill Top Cl. *LS24: Stut 6C 54*
(off Green La.)
Hill Vw. YO31: York 6A **20**
Hinton Av. YO24: York 1E **37**
HMP Askham Grange
YO23: Ask R 4F **35**
Hobgate YO24: York 4F **27**
Hob Moor Dr. YO24: York 5G **27**
Hob Moor Ter. YO24: York 6H **27**
Hobson Cl. YO23: Cop 2C **44**
Hodgson La. YO26: Up P 5A **16**
Holburns Cft. YO10: H'tn 6H **29**
Holden Gdns. YO8: Sel 3A **58**
HOLGATE 4G **27**
Holgate Bri. Gdns. YO24: York . . .4A **28**
Holgate Lodge Dr. YO26: York 3G **27**
Holgate Pk. YO26: York 3H **27**
Holgate Pk. Dr. YO26: York 3H **27**
Holgate Rd. YO24: York 4H **27**
Hollands Rd. YO10: York 6E **29**
Hollies, The YO8: Osg 5H **57**
Hollis Cres. YO32: Stre 5A **6**
Holly Bank YO26: Up P 5A **16**
YO41: Elv 5F **43**
Holly Bank Gro. YO24: York 5H **27**
Holly Bank Rd. YO24: York 5H **27**
Holly Cl. YO23: Aca M 4H **45**
Holly Gro. YO8: Sel 4C **58**
Holly Ter. YO10: York 6D **28**
Holly Tree Cft. YO19: Dun 1A **32**
Holly Tree Gth. YO32: Stock F 6F **13**
Holly Tree La. YO19: Dun 1A **32**
YO32: Hax 3D **10**
Hollytree Wlk. YO26: Tad 5C **54**
Hollytree Way YO8: Bray 6A **58**
Hollywood YO8: Sel 1C **58**
Holmefield Cl. YO8: Bray 6B **58**
Holmefield Ct. YO8: Bray 6B **58**
Holmefield La. YO10: H'tn 6G **29**
Holme Hill La. YO10: H'tn 2D **40**
Holme La. YO8: Sel 1E **59**
Holme Lea YO32: Stre 5H **5**
Holmes Av. YO8: Sel 1D **58**
Holmes Dr. YO19: Ric 2B **56**
Holroyd Av. YO31: York 2G **29**
HOLTBY 4B **22**
Holtby La. YO19: Holt 3D **20**
Holyrood Dr. YO30: York 2F **17**
Homefield Cl. YO23: Cop 1C **44**
Home Front Experience, The *2E 31*
(off Murton La.)
Homestead Cl. YO32: Hunt 4F **19**
Honeysuckle Cl. YO8: Sel 5D **58**
Honeysuckle Ho. YO24: York 1F **37**
Honley Ho. *YO31: York 1D 28*
(off Abbot St.)
Hope St. YO10: York 5G **3** (4D **28**)
Hopewell Ter. YO41: Elv 5F **43**
Hopgrove La. Nth. YO32: York 2A **20**
Hopgrove La. Sth. YO32: York 2B **20**
Hopgrove Sports Complex 2A **20**
Horbury Ho. *YO31: York 1D 28*
(off Garden St.)
Hornbeam Cl. YO30: York 3B **18**
Hornbys Pas. *YO1: York 2D 2*
(off Stonegate)
Horner St. YO30: York 6B **18**
Hornsey Gth. YO32: Wigg 2C **10**
Horseman Av. YO23: Cop 6C **36**
Horseman Cl. YO23: Cop 6C **36**
Horseman Ct. YO23: Cop 6C **36**
Horseman Dr. YO23: Cop 6C **36**
Horseman La. YO23: Cop 6C **36**
Horseshoe, The YO24: York 2G **37**
Horsfield Way YO19: Dun 1A **32**
Horsman Av. YO10: York . . .6G **3** (4E **29**)
Hospital Flds. YO10: York 6D **28**
Hospital Flds. Rd. YO10: York 6D **28**
Hotham Av. YO26: York 5D **26**
Hotham's Ct. YO1: York 4G **3**
Houndsway YO24: York 1D **36**
Howard Dr. YO30: York 3F **17**
Howard Link YO30: York 3F **17**
Howard Rd. YO32: Stre 5A **6**
Howard St. YO10: York 5D **28**
Howden La. YO19: Crock H, Nab . . .3C **46**
Howden Rd. YO8: B'by 5F **57**
Howe Hill Cl. YO26: York 3G **27**
Howe Hill Rd. YO26: York 3G **27**
Howe St. YO24: York 4F **27**
Hubert St. YO23: York 6B **28**
Huby Ct. YO1: York 5H **3** (4E **29**)
Hudson Cl. YO26: Tad 1E **55**
YO41: Stam B 5H **23**
Hudson Cres. YO30: York 6A **18**
Hudson Vw. YO26: Tad 1E **55**
Hudson Way YO26: Neth P 5E **17**
YO26: Tad 2E **55**
Hull Rd. YO8: Osg 5G **57**
YO10: York 4F **29**
YO19: Dun, Grim, York 3E **31**
Humber Dr. YO32: Stre 5A **6**
Hungate YO1: York 3F **3** (3D **28**)
(not continuous)
Hunt Ct. YO1: York 2F **3** (2D **28**)
Hunter Dr. YO41: Elv 5C **42**
Hunters Cl. YO19: Dun 2G **31**
YO32: Hax 3C **10**
Hunters Way YO8: Sel 3C **58**
YO24: York 2H **37**
Hunterswood Way YO19: Dun 2H **31**
HUNTINGTON 2F **19**
Huntington M. YO31: York 6D **18**
Huntington Rd.
YO31: York 1G **3** (1D **28**)
YO32: Hunt 2E **19**
Huntington Stadium 3F **19**
Huntsmans La. YO41: Stam B 2H **23**
Huntsmans Wlk. YO24: York 6D **26**
Hurricane Way YO30: York 2G **17**
Hurst's Yd. YO1: York 4G **3** (3D **28**)
Hutchinson St. YO8: Sel 1C **58**
Hutton Cl. YO26: Neth P 3C **16**
Hutton Dr. YO26: Hut W 6A **24**
Hutton Hall Farm Cotts.
YO26: Hut W 6A **24**
HUTTON WANDESLEY 6A **24**
Hyrst Gro. YO31: York 1E **29**

I

Ikin Way YO32: Hunt 5F **11**
Ilton Gth. YO30: York 3A **18**
Imperial Ct. YO30: York 5B **18**
Ingleborough Av. YO10: York 3H **29**
Ingleby Dr. YO26: Tad 2E **55**
Ingleton Ho. *YO26: York 3G 27*
(off Burnsall Dr.)
Ingleton Wlk. YO31: York 2G **29**
Ingram Av. YO30: York 5C **18**
Ingram Ct. YO10: H'tn 1H **39**
Ings Cl. YO8: B'by 5F **57**
Ings Flats YO10: Ful 2D **38**
Ings La. YO8: Wist L 3E **57**
YO19: Thor 6E **51**
YO26: Neth P 4D **16**
Ings Roods La. YO8: B'by 5F **57**
Ings Vw. YO30: York 3F **17**

A-Z York 65

Ingsway—Lowther Ter.

Ingsway YO30: York ... 5A 18
Inholmes La. YO26: Tad ... 3C 54
Inman Ter. YO26: York ... 3F 27
Innisfree Glade YO19: Whel ... 4C 50
Innovation Cen. YO10: H'tn ... 5H 29
Innovation Cl. YO10: H'tn ... 5H 29
Innovation Way YO10: H'tn ... 5H 29
Intake Av. YO30: York ... 5C 18
Intake La. YO19: Dun ... 2A 32
YO23: Aca M ... 6F 45
Invicta Ct. YO24: York ... 1E 37
Irvine Way YO24: York ... 2D 36
Irwin Av. YO31: York ... 1E 29
Iver Cl. YO26: York ... 2E 27
Ivy Pl. YO32: New E ... 2D 18

J

Jackson St. YO31: York ... 1D 28
Jacob Ct. YO1: York ... 4C 2
Jacobi Cl. YO30: York ... 6A 18
Jacobs Ct. YO30: York ... 6A 18
James Backhouse Pl.
YO24: York ... 4G 27
James Nicolson Link
YO30: York ... 3A 18
James St. YO8: Sel ... 2D 58
YO10: York ... 2H **3** (2E **29**)
James St. Ind. Est.
YO10: York ... 4H **3** (3E **29**)
James St. Travellers' Site
YO10: York ... 2H **3** (3E **29**)
James Way YO10: H'tn ... 6G 29
Jamieson Ter. YO23: York ... 6B 28
Janus Ho. *YO10: York ... 4F 29*
(off Olympian Ct.)
Jasmine Cl. YO32: New E ... 3D 18
Jasmine Gth. YO41: Sutt D ... 6H 43
Jaywick Cl. YO32: Stre ... 2B 6
Jedwell Cl. YO32: New E ... 6D 10
Jennifer Gro. YO24: York ... 5H 27
Jervaulx Ho. *YO10: York ... 4F 29*
(off Lawrence Sq.)
Jervis Ct. YO41: Sutt D ... 6H 43
Jervis Rd. YO24: York ... 1G 37
Jewbury YO31: York ... 2F **3** (2D **28**)
JJB Fitness
Selby ... 4E 59
Jockey La. YO32: Hunt ... 3F 19
John Burrill Homes YO30: York ... 6A 18
John Saville Ct. *YO1: York ... 2F 3*
(off Ogleforth)
Johnson St. YO8: Sel ... 1C 58
John St. YO8: Sel ... 1E 59
YO31: York ... 1E 29
John Ward Cl. YO41: Stam B ... 5H 23
Jorvik Cl. YO26: York ... 2E 27
Jorvik Viking Cen. ... 4E 3 (3C 28)
Joseph Rowntree Theatre ... 5D 18
Jubbergate YO1: York ... 3E **3** (3C **28**)
Jubilee Ct. YO32: Hax ... 3D 10
Jubilee Ter. YO26: York ... 2H 27
Julia Av. YO32: Hunt ... 3H 19
Julia Av. Retail Pk.
YO32: Hunt ... 3G 19
Juniper Cl. YO32: New E ... 2D 18
Juno Ho. *YO10: York ... 4F 29*
(off Olympian Ct.)
Jupiter Ho. *YO10: York ... 4F 29*
(off Olympian Ct.)
Jute Rd. YO26: York ... 2D 26

K

Kathryn Av. YO32: Hunt ... 3G 19
Kaye Dr. YO8: Osg ... 5G 57
Keats Cl. YO30: York ... 5H 17
Keble Cl. YO23: Bish ... 6B 38
Keble Dr. YO23: Bish ... 6A 38
Keble Gdns. YO23: Bish ... 1B 46
Keble Pk. Cres. YO23: Bish ... 6A 38
Keble Pk. Nth. YO23: Bish ... 6A 38
Keble Pk. Sth. YO23: Bish ... 6A 38
Keepers Way YO19: Dun ... 1B 32
Keith Av. YO32: Hunt ... 1G 19
Kelcbar Cl. YO26: Tad ... 2C 54
Kelcbar Hill YO26: Tad ... 2B 54
Kelcbar Way YO26: Tad ... 2C 54
Keldale YO32: Hax ... 1E 11
Kelfield Ct. YO19: Ric ... 3A 56
Kelfield Rd. YO19: Ric ... 3A 56
Kempton Cl. YO24: York ... 6F 27
Kendal Cl. YO19: Dun ... 1A 32
Kendrew Cl. YO32: Hunt ... 2F 19
Kenlay Cl. YO32: New E ... 1D 18
Kennedy Dr. YO32: Hax ... 2D 10
Kenrick Ct. YO1: York ... 3F 3
Kenrick Pl. YO26: York ... 2E 27
Kensal Ri. YO10: York ... 5D 28
Kensington Ct. YO24: York ... 1H 37
Kensington Ho.
YO26: York ... 2A **2** (2A **28**)
Kensington Rd. YO30: York ... 3F 17
Kensington St. YO23: York ... 6B 28
Kentmere Dr. YO30: York ... 4H 17
Kent Rd. YO8: Sel ... 1B 58
Kent St. YO10: York ... 6F **3** (4D **28**)
Kerrside YO30: York ... 5G 17
Kerver La. YO19: Dun ... 1A 32
Kestrel Wood Way YO31: York ... 3F 19
Keswick Way YO32: Hunt ... 6F 11
Kettlestring La. YO30: York ... 3A 18
Kettlewell La. YO26: Neth P ... 4F 15
KEXBY ... 4G 33
Kexby Av. YO10: York ... 4F 29
Kexby Stray YO19: Dun ... 1B 42
Key Way YO19: Ful ... 4F 39
Kilburn Ho. *YO31: York ... 1D 28*
(off Lowther St.)
Kilburn Rd. YO10: York ... 5D 28
Kimberlow Woods Hill
YO10: York ... 4A 30
Kinbrace Dr. YO24: York ... 2D 36
Kingfisher Cl. YO32: Hunt ... 6F 11
Kingfisher Ho. YO10: York ... 5H 3
King Rudding Cl. YO19: Ric ... 3B 56
King Rudding La. YO19: Ric ... 3C 56
Kings Acre YO31: York ... 1H 29
Kingsclere YO32: Hunt ... 5F 11
Kings Cl. YO8: B'by ... 3F 57
King's Ct. YO1: York ... 3E **3** (3C **28**)
Kings Gth. YO41: Stam B ... 5H 23
Kingsland Ter. YO26: York ... 2H 27
King's Manor, The ... 2C 2
Kings Moor Rd. YO32: Stock F ... 1E 21
King's Sq. YO1: York ... 3E **3** (3C **28**)
King's Staith YO1: York ... 4E **3** (3C **28**)
Kingsthorpe YO24: York ... 5F 27
King St. YO1: York ... 4E **3** (3C **28**)
Kingsway YO41: Stam B ... 4H 23
Kingsway Nth. YO30: York ... 6A 18
Kingsway W. YO24: York ... 5F 27
Kingswood Gro. YO24: York ... 5F 27
Kir Cres. YO24: York ... 4E 27
Kirkby Av. YO8: Sel ... 1C 58
Kirkcroft YO32: Wigg ... 3C 10
Kirkdale Rd. YO10: Osb ... 3B 30
Kirkgate YO26: Tad ... 3E 55
Kirkham Av. YO31: York ... 5E 19
Kirkland Cl. YO8: Sel ... 3E 59
Kirklands YO32: Stre ... 5A 6
Kirkstall Ho. *YO10: York ... 4F 29*
(off Nicholas Gdns.)
Kirkstone Dr. YO31: York ... 1G 29
Kirk Vw. YO26: York ... 4E 27
Kirkwell YO23: Bish ... 5A 38
Kitchen Dr. YO8: Sel ... 3E 59
Kitchener Cl. YO8: Sel ... 1C 58
Kitchener St. YO8: Sel ... 1C 58
YO31: York ... 6D 18
Kitemere Pl. YO24: York ... 1D 36
KitKat Crescent ... 6B 18
Kitty Gth. YO19: Whel ... 5C 50
KNAPTON ... 2C 26
Knapton Cl. YO32: Stre ... 5A 6
Knapton La. YO26: York ... 3D 26
KNAVESMIRE ... 6B 28
Knavesmire Cres. YO23: York ... 6B 28
Knavesmire Rd. YO23: York ... 5A 28
Knoll, The YO24: York ... 5D 26
Kyle Way YO26: Neth P ... 5D 16
Kyme St. YO1: York ... 5D **2** (4C **28**)

L

Laburnum Cl. YO23: Ruff ... 3D 24
Laburnum Farm Cl.
YO26: Hess ... 6C 14
Laburnum Gth. YO31: York ... 5F 19
Lady Anne Ct. YO1: York ... 5D 2
Lady Flat La. LS24: Col ... 5A 44
Lady Hamilton Gdns.
YO24: York ... 5G 27
Lady Hewley's Cotts.
YO1: York ... 3F **3** (3D **28**)
Lady Mill Gth. YO30: York ... 5B 18
Lady Peckett's Yd.
YO1: York ... 4F **3** (3D **28**)
Lady Rd. YO30: York ... 6B 18
Ladysmith M. YO32: Stre ... 4H 5
Lady Wortley Pl. YO23: Mid ... 3C 38
Lakeside YO23: Aca M ... 5G 45
Lakeside Ct. YO24: York ... 1H 37
Lakeside Gdns. YO32: Stre ... 2B 6
Lambert Ct. YO1: York ... 5D **2** (4C **28**)
Lamel Hill ... 5E 29
Lamel St. YO10: York ... 4G 29
Lamplugh Cres. YO23: Bish ... 6B 38
Lancar Cl. YO32: Wigg ... 2A 10
Lancaster Pk. YO30: York ... 2A 18
Lancaster Way YO30: York ... 4A 18
Landalewood Rd. YO30: York ... 3H 17
Landau Cl. YO30: York ... 5H 17
Landing Cl. YO8: B'by ... 5F 57
Landing La. YO8: B'by ... 5E 57
YO19: Ric ... 4A 56
YO26: York ... 2G 27
YO32: Hax ... 5E 11
Landings, The YO32: Hax ... 2F 11
Lane, The YO41: Gate H ... 2D 22
Lang Av. YO10: York ... 3G 29
Langdale Av. YO31: York ... 1H 29
Langdale Gro. YO8: Sel ... 4C 58
Langholme Dr. YO26: York ... 1E 27
Langley Ct. YO32: Hunt ... 5F 11
Lang Rd. YO23: Bish ... 5H 37
YO32: Hunt ... 5F 11
Langsett Gro. YO30: York ... 2H 17
Langton Ct. YO24: York ... 6B 2
YO32: Stre ... 5H 5
Langwith Stray YO10: H'tn ... 6D 40
Lansdowne Ter. YO10: York ... 4E 29
Lansdown Way YO32: Hax ... 2E 11
Lanshaw Cft. YO30: York ... 4H 17
Larches, The YO41: Elv ... 5G 43
Larchfield YO31: York ... 6H 19
Larch Way YO32: Hax ... 1D 10
Larkfield Cl. YO23: Cop ... 6C 36
Larkfield Rd. YO8: Sel ... 3B 58
Lasenby Cl. YO32: New E ... 6D 10
Lastingham Ter. YO10: York ... 5D 28
Laurel Cl. YO32: Ear ... 4G 11
Laurence Gro. YO8: Sel ... 4E 59
Laurie Backhouse Ct. *YO8: Sel ... 2D 58*
(off Harper St.)
Lavender Gro. YO26: York ... 2G 27
Laveracks Ind. Est. YO41: Elv ... 4D 42
Lawnswood Dr. YO30: York ... 5H 17
Lawnway YO31: York ... 6G 19
Lawrence Ct. YO10: York ... 5H 3
Lawrence La. YO10: York ... 6H 3
Lawrence Sq. YO10: York ... 4F 29
Lawrence St.
YO10: York ... 5H **3** (4E **29**)
Lawson Rd. YO24: York ... 2H 37
LAYERTHORPE ... 2H **3** (2E **29**)
Layerthorpe YO31: York ... 2G **3** (2D **28**)
Leadley Cft. YO23: Cop ... 2C 44
Leadmill La. YO1: York ... 5F **3** (4D **28**)
Leake St. YO10: York ... 5H **3** (4E **29**)
Learmans Way YO23: Cop ... 6E 37
Lea Way YO32: Hunt ... 1G 19
Leeds Rd. YO8: Sel ... 3A 58
YO26: Tad ... 3C 54
Leeman Rd. YO26: York ... 2A **2** (2H **27**)
Leeside YO24: York ... 1G 37
Leicester Way *YO1: York ... 5F 3*
(off Ancroft Cl.)
Leighton Cft. YO30: York ... 4H 17
Lendal YO1: York ... 3D **2** (3C **28**)
Lendal Bri. YO1: York ... 3D 2
Lerecroft Rd. YO24: York ... 1F 37
Lesley Av. YO10: York ... 1E 39
Leven Rd. YO24: York ... 2F 37
Levisham St. YO10: York ... 5D 28
Leyes, The YO10: Osb ... 3A 30
Leyfield Cl. YO32: Stre ... 4H 5
Leyland Rd. YO31: York ... 1G 29
Liber Ho. *YO10: York ... 4F 29*
(off Olympian Ct.)
Library Sq. YO1: York ... 2D 2
Lichfield Ct. YO23: York ... 6B 28
Lidgett Gro. YO26: York ... 1D 26
Lilac Av. YO10: York ... 4H 29
YO23: Aca M ... 6G 45
Lilac Gro. YO32: New E ... 1D 18
Lilbourne Dr. YO30: York ... 5A 18
Lilling Av. YO31: York ... 5F 19
Lime Av. YO31: York ... 6F 19
Limegarth YO26: Up P ... 4B 16
Limes, The YO32: Stock F ... 1E 21
Limes Ct. YO31: York ... 1F 29
Lime Tree Av. YO32: New E ... 2D 18
Lime Tree Gdns. YO8: Sel ... 1B 58
Lime Tree Gro. YO8: Sel ... 1B 58
Lime Tree M. YO19: Dun ... 1A 32
Lincoln St. YO26: York ... 2H 27
Lindale YO24: York ... 2E 37
Linden Cl. YO32: Hunt ... 6F 11
Linden Gro. YO30: York ... 5A 18
Lindley Ct. YO10: H'tn ... 1H 39
Lindley Rd. YO30: York ... 4H 17
Lindley St. YO24: York ... 4H 27
Lindley Wood Gro.
YO30: York ... 2G 17
Lindsey Av. YO26: York ... 3F 27
Lingcroft La. YO19: Ful ... 6E 39
Lingfield Cres. YO24: York ... 6H 27
Link, The YO8: Sel ... 3B 58
YO10: York ... 1E 39
YO23: Cop ... 6C 36
Link Av. YO30: York ... 5C 18
Link Bus. Pk. YO10: Osb ... 3C 30
Link Rd. YO10: Osb ... 3B 30
YO32: Hunt ... 3D 18
Link Rd. Ct. YO10: Osb ... 3B 30
Links, The YO26: Tad ... 4D 54
Linley Av. YO32: Hax ... 2E 11
Linnet Way YO24: York ... 1E 37
Linton Rd. YO26: Neth P ... 4C 16
Linton St. YO26: York ... 2G 27
Lister Way YO30: York ... 6A 18
Little Av. YO30: York ... 5B 18
Lit. Catterton La. YO26: Tad ... 1H 55
Littlefield Cl. YO26: Neth P ... 3B 16
Little Gth. YO26: Neth P ... 3C 16
Lit. Grimston Cotts.
YO26: Stut ... 6D 54
Lit. Hallfield Rd.
YO31: York ... 2H **3** (2E **29**)
Little La. YO32: Hax ... 2D 10
Little Mdws. YO32: Hax ... 3D 10
Little Shambles *YO1: York ... 3E 3*
(off Shambles)
Little Stonegate
YO1: York ... 2D **2** (3C **28**)
Littlethorpe Cl. YO32: Stre ... 2B 6
Livingstone St. YO26: York ... 2H 27
Lloyd Cl. YO10: H'tn ... 6H 29
Lob La. YO41: Stam B ... 5H 23
Lochrin Pl. YO26: York ... 3D 26
Lockey Cft. YO32: Wigg ... 3C 10
Lock Ho. La. YO32: Ear ... 3F 11
Lockwood St.
YO31: York ... 1F **3** (2D **28**)
Lockyer Cl. YO30: York ... 5A 18
Londesborough St. YO8: Sel ... 2D 58
Long Cl. La.
YO10: York ... 5G **3** (4D **28**)
Longcroft YO32: Wigg ... 1C 10
Longfield Ter.
YO30: York ... 2B **2** (2B **28**)
Long Furrow YO32: Hax ... 3C 10
Long La. YO10: H'tn ... 2C 40
YO41: Kex ... 4H 33
Long Mann Hills Rd. YO8: Sel ... 4C 58
Long Ridge Dr. YO26: Up P ... 4C 16
Long Ridge Gdns. YO26: Up P ... 4B 16
Long Ridge La.
YO26: Neth P, Up P ... 4B 16
Long Trods YO8: Sel ... 1D 58
Longwood Link YO30: York ... 2G 17
Longwood Rd. YO30: York ... 3H 17
Lord Mayor's Wlk.
YO31: York ... 1E **3** (2C **28**)
Lords La. YO26: Neth P ... 1F 15
Lords Moor La. YO32: Stre ... 3B 6
Loriners Dr. YO23: Cop ... 6D 36
Lorne St. YO23: York ... 6B 28
Lorraine Av. YO41: Elv ... 5F 43
Lorrenger La. YO23: Ask B ... 2B 36
Love La. YO10: York ... 1C 38
YO24: York ... 6A **2** (4A **28**)
Lovel Ho. YO24: York ... 1F 37
Lovell St. YO23: York ... 5C 28
Low Cft. YO32: Stre ... 4H 5
Lwr. Darnborough St.
YO23: York ... 6E **3** (4C **28**)
Lwr. Ebor St. YO23: York ... 6E **3** (5C **28**)
Lower Friargate
YO1: York ... 4E **3** (3C **28**)
Lwr. Priory St.
YO1: York ... 5C **2** (4B **28**)
Loweswater Rd. YO30: York ... 4G 17
LOW FIELD ... 5E 27
Lowfield Dr. YO32: Hax ... 1D 10
Lowfield La. YO26: Knap ... 3B 26
Lowfield Rd. YO8: B'by ... 4G 57
Lowfields Dr. YO24: York ... 4E 27
Low Grn. YO23: Cop ... 1D 44
Lowick YO24: York ... 2E 37
Low La. YO10: H'tn ... 6H 29
Low Mdw. YO8: Sel ... 1D 58
Low Mill Cl. YO10: York ... 4B 30
Low Moor Av. YO10: York ... 2F 39
Low Moor La. YO23: Ang ... 2E 35
YO26: Hess ... 6D 14
Lown Hill YO24: York ... 5E 27
Low Ousegate
YO1: York ... 4D **2** (3C **28**)
Low Petergate
YO1: York ... 2E **3** (2C **28**)
Low Poppleton La. YO26: York ... 6D 16
Lowther Ct. YO31: York ... 1D 28
Lowther Dr. YO8: Sel ... 4F 59
Lowther St. YO31: York ... 1C 28
Lowther Ter. YO24: York ... 5A **2** (4A **28**)

Low Well La.—Munster Ho.

Low Well La. YO19: Whel 5B 50
Low Well Pk. YO19: Whel 5B 50
Low Westfield Rd.
YO23: Cop 2A 44
Loxley Cl. YO30: York 3H 17
Lucas Av. YO30: York 5C 18
Lucerne Cl. YO19: Ric 2B 56
Lucombe Way YO32: New E 1D 18
Lumley Rd. YO30: York 6B 18
Lund Cl. YO32: Wigg 3C 10
Lunds Ct. YO1: York 3E 3
Lundy Cl. YO30: York 4A 18
Lycett Rd. YO24: York 2H 37
Lydham Ct. YO24: York 1E 37
Lyndale Av. YO10: Osb 4A 30
Lynden Way YO24: York 4F 27
Lynton Cl. YO8: Bray 6C 58
Lynton Gdns. YO8: Bray 6C 58
Lynwood Av. YO23: Cop 6C 36
Lynwood Cl. YO32: Stre 4H 5
Lynwood Vw. YO23: Cop 6C 36
Lysander Cl. YO30: York 3A 18

M

McArthur Glen Designer Outlet Village
YO19: Ful 5D 38
McHugh Ct. YO10: H'tn 1H 39
Maclagan Rd. YO23: Bish 5H 37
McQuades Ct. YO1: York 5H 3
Magazine Rd. YO8: Sel 6F 57
Magnolia Gro. YO32: New E 3D 18
Maida Gro. YO10: York 5D 28
Main Av. YO31: York 2F 29
Main St. YO10: Ful 1D 38
YO10: H'tn 6G 29
YO19: Dei 6H 47
YO19: Esc 3F 53
YO19: Nab 3B 46
YO19: Ric 3B 56
YO19: Whel 5A 50
YO23: Ask B 4H 35
YO23: Bish 5A 38
YO23: Cop 1C 44
YO26: Hess 6B 14
YO26: Knap 2B 26
YO26: Neth P, Up P 3A 16
YO30: Ship 1A 8
YO41: Elv 5F 43
(not continuous)
YO41: Stam B 4G 23
Malbys Gro. YO23: Cop 1D 44
Malham Gro. YO31: York 2H 29
Mallard Way YO32: Hax 2E 11
Mallory Cl. YO32: New E 1D 18
Maltings Ct. YO8: Sel 1D 58
Malt Kiln Ter. YO26: Stut 6C 54
Malton Av. YO31: York 1E 29
Malton Rd. YO31: York 1F 29
YO32: York 4H 19
Malton Way YO30: York 5H 17
Malt Shovel Ct.
YO1: York 4F 3 (3D 28)
Malvern Av. YO26: York 3F 27
Malvern Cl. YO32: Hunt 6G 11
Mancroft YO32: Hax 3C 10
Manley Cl. YO32: New E 1D 18
Manor Beeches, The
YO19: Dun 1H 31
Manor Cl. YO26: Up P 5B 16
Manor Ct. YO10: York 4F 29
YO26: Up P 5B 16
YO32: Hunt 5F 11
YO41: Stam B 4G 23
Manor Dr. YO19: Dun 2H 31
Manor Dr. Nth. YO26: York 3F 27
Manor Dr. Sth. YO26: York 3F 27
Mnr. Farm Cl. YO8: Bray 6B 58
YO23: Cop 1C 44
Manor Gth. YO19: Ric 3B 56
YO32: Wigg 3B 10
Manor Heath YO23: Cop 6B 36
Manor La. YO30: York 3F 17
Manor Pk. Cl. YO30: York 3G 17
Manor Pk. Gro. YO30: York 3G 17
Manor Pk. Rd. YO30: York 3F 17
Manor Rd. YO26: Stut 6D 54
YO26: Tad 2E 55
Manor Way YO30: York 3G 17
Mansfield Ho. *YO31: York 1C 28*
(off Lowther St.)
Mansfield St.
YO31: York 2G 3 (2D 28)
Mansion House 3D 2
Manthorpe Wlk.
YO26: York 3G 27
Maple Av. YO23: Bish 6A 38
Maple Ct. YO10: Ful 3E 39
YO32: Stock F 6F 13
Maple Gro. YO8: Bray 6A 58
YO10: York 6C 28
Maplehurst Av. YO31: York 6D 18
Maple Tree Av. YO8: B'by 5F 57
Maplewood Paddock
YO24: York 6E 27
March St. YO31: York 1D 28
Margaret Philipson Ct.
YO1: York 2F 3
(off Aldwark)
Margaret St.
YO10: York 5G 3 (4D 28)
Marigold Cl. YO8: Sel 5D 58
Marjorie Waite Ct. YO30: York 5B 18
Market Cross YO8: Sel 2D 58
Market La. YO8: Sel 2D 58
Market Pl. YO8: Sel 2D 58
Market Sq. YO10: H'tn 5G 29
Market St. YO1: York 3E 3 (3C 28)
Mkt. Weighton Rd. YO8: B'by 2G 57
Markham Cres. YO31: York 1C 28
Markham St. YO31: York 1D 28
Marlborough Av. YO26: Tad 4C 54
Marlborough Cl. YO30: York 2F 17
Marlborough Dr. YO26: Tad 4C 54
Marlborough Gro.
YO10: York 6F 3 (5D 28)
Marlborough Vs. *YO10: York 5D 28*
(off Sandringham St.)
Marlborough Wharf
YO10: York 6F 3 (5D 28)
(off Marlborough Gro.)
Marmiam Dr. YO32: Stock F 1E 21
Marquis Ct. YO26: York 1F 27
Marsden Pk. YO30: York 3A 18
Marston Av. YO26: York 4D 26
Marston Cres. YO26: York 4D 26
Marston La.
YO26: Hess, Moor M 6A 14
Martello Way YO32: Hunt 4G 19
Marten Cl. YO30: York 5A 18
Martin Cheeseman Ct.
YO24: York 1E 37
Martins Ct. YO26: York 2A 28
Marygate YO30: York 2C 2 (2B 28)
Marygate La.
YO30: York 1B 2 (2B 28)
Mask La. YO41: Kex 1H 43
Massey St. YO8: Sel 2D 58
Matmer Ct. YO10: York 4F 29
Mattison Way YO24: York 5G 27
Mawsons Ct. YO1: York 4F 3
Mayfair Ho. YO1: York 5F 3
Mayfield Ct. YO24: York 1H 37
Mayfield Dr. YO8: Bray 6B 58
Mayfield Gro. YO24: York 1G 37
Mayfield Rd. YO8: Bray 6B 58
Mayfield Ter. YO26: Tad 2F 55
Maypole Gro. YO19: Nab 3B 46
Maythorn Rd. YO31: York 3F 19
Maythorpe YO23: Ruff 3D 24
Meadlands YO31: York 1H 29
Meadowbeck Cl. YO10: Osb 3H 29
Meadow Ct. YO24: York 1G 37
Meadow Cft. YO8: Bray 5B 58
Meadowfields Dr. YO31: York 3E 19
Meadow Gth. YO26: Tad 2F 55
Meadow La. YO32: Hax 3D 10
Meadow Pl. YO8: Sel 1C 58
Meadow Ri. YO26: Tad 1F 55
Meadows, The YO19: Ric 3A 56
YO30: Ske 6D 8
Meadow Wlk. YO26: Tad 2F 55
Meadow Way YO26: Tad 2F 55
YO31: York 6F 19
YO32: Hunt 1F 19
Meadway YO8: Sel 3A 58
Meadway Cres. YO8: Sel 3A 58
Meadway Dr. YO8: Sel 3A 58
Meam Cl. YO10: Osb 3B 30
Medway Ho. YO10: York 5G 3
Megabowl
York 1A 18
Melander Cl. YO26: York 3D 26
Melander Gdns. YO32: Hax 4D 10
Melbourne Ct. YO10: York 6G 3
Melbourne St.
YO10: York 6G 3 (5D 28)
Melcombe Av. YO32: Stre 4H 5
Melodies Driving Range 2B 18
Melrose Cl. YO31: York 2F 29
Melrosegate YO10: York 4F 29
YO31: York 1F 29
Melroses Yd. YO1: York 4G 3
Melton Av. YO30: York 5H 17
Melton Dr. YO23: Bish 6A 38
YO30: York 5H 17
Melwood Gro. YO26: York 2D 26
Mendip Cl. YO32: Hunt 6F 11
Merchant Ga. YO1: York 3D 28
Merchantgate
YO1: York 4F 3 (3D 28)
Merchants Adventurers Hall
.....4F 3 (3D 28)
Merchants Ct.
YO31: York 1H 3 (2E 29)
Merchant Taylors Hall 2F 3
Merchant Way YO23: Cop 6D 36
Merewood Cl. YO31: Ear 4G 11
Merlin Covert YO31: York 2F 19
Merton Ct. YO24: York 5G 27
Metcalfe La. YO10: Osb 2A 30
YO31: Osb 2A 30
Micklegate YO1: York 5C 2 (3B 28)
YO8: Sel 1D 58
Micklegate Bar Mus. 5C 2 (4B 28)
Middle Banks YO32: Wigg 2C 10
Middlebrook Gdns. YO8: Bray 6B 58
Middlecroft Dr. YO32: Stre 4H 5
Middlecroft Gro. YO32: Stre 4A 6
Middleham Av. YO31: York 5E 19
Middle La. YO8: Bray 6D 58
MIDDLETHORPE 3B 38
Middlethorpe Dr. YO24: York 2G 37
Middlethorpe Gro.
YO24: York 2H 37
Middleton Ho. YO1: York 5E 3
Middleton Rd. YO24: York 5F 27
Middlewood Cl. YO23: Ruff 3D 24
Midgley Cl. YO41: Stam B 5H 23
Midway Av. YO26: Neth P 4C 16
Mildred Gro. YO24: York 5H 27
Milennium Bridge
York 6C 28
Milestone Av. YO23: Ruff 4D 24
Milford M. YO32: Hax 4D 10
Milford Way YO32: Hax 4D 10
Millcroft YO8: Bray 6A 58
Millennium Ct. YO31: York 2H 3
Millers Cft. YO23: Cop 6D 36
Millfield Av. YO10: York 4F 29
Millfield Bus. Cen.
YO26: Neth P 5D 16
Millfield Ct. YO19: Whel 5B 50
Millfield Gdns. YO26: Neth P 3C 16
Millfield Ind. Est.
YO19: Whel 6A 50
Millfield La. YO10: York 4G 29
YO26: Neth P 3C 16
Millfield Rd. YO23: York 5B 28
Millgate YO8: Sel 1D 58
(not continuous)
Millgate M. YO8: Sel 1D 58
Millgates YO26: York 1E 27
Mill Hill YO19: Esc 3H 53
Mill Hill Dr. YO32: Hunt 1F 19
Mill La. YO8: Bray 6A 58
YO19: Ric 2B 56
YO23: Ask B 5B 36
YO23: Ask R 5D 34
YO23: Ruff 6A 14
YO26: Hess 6A 14
YO26: Stut 6D 54
YO26: Tad 2E 55
YO31: York 1E 29
YO32: Wigg 2A 10
Mill Mt. YO24: York 6A 2 (4A 28)
Mill Mt. Ct. YO24: York 6A 2 (4A 28)
Mill St. YO1: York 5F 3 (4D 28)
Milner St. YO24: York 4F 27
Milson Gro. YO10: York 4G 29
Milton Carr YO30: York 4H 17
Milton St. YO10: York 4F 29
Minchin Cl. YO30: York 4B 18
Minerva Ho. *YO10: York 4F 29*
(off Olympian Ct.)
Minster Av. YO31: York 3F 19
Minster Cl. YO32: Wigg 2C 10
Minster Ct. YO1: York 1E 3 (2C 28)
Minster Gates
YO1: York 2E 3 (2C 28)
Minster Vw. YO32: Wigg 3C 10
Minster Yd. YO1: York 2E 3 (2C 28)
(Deangate)
YO1: York 1E 3 (2C 28)
(Minster Ct.)
Minter Cl. YO24: York 6D 26
Mirkhill Rd. YO8: Sel 1C 58
Mistral Ct. YO31: York 6E 19
Mitchell Way YO30: York 2G 17
Mitchel's La. YO10: York 1F 39
Miterdale YO24: York 2E 37
Moatfield YO10: Osb 3A 30
Moatside Ct. YO31: York 1E 3 (2C 28)
Moat Way YO8: Bray 5A 58
Moins Ct. YO10: Osb 3B 30
Moiser Cl. YO32: New E 1D 18
Monarch Way YO26: York 1F 27
Monk Av. YO31: York 6F 19
Monk Bar Ct. YO1: York 1F 3 (2C 28)
Monkbridge Ct.
YO31: York 1G 3 (1D 28)
Monkgate YO31: York 1F 3 (2D 28)
Monkgate Cloisters
YO31: York 1F 3 (2D 28)
Monks Cross Dr. YO32: Hunt 2H 19
Monks Cross Link YO32: Hunt 6H 11
Monks Cross Shop. Pk.
YO32: Hunt 2H 19
MONK STRAY 6E 19
Monkton Rd. YO31: York 5E 19
Monroe Cl. YO30: York 3G 17
Montague Rd. YO23: Bish 6A 38
Montague St. YO23: York 6C 28
Montague Wlk. YO26: Up P 3B 16
Montrose Av. YO31: York 5D 18
Monument Cl. YO24: York 4G 27
YO26: York 4G 27
Moor Carr La. YO8: B'by 3F 57
(not continuous)
Moor Cl. YO19: Whel 4B 50
Moorcroft Rd. YO24: York 2F 37
Moore Av. YO10: York 3H 29
MOOR END
YO23 .....3H 45
YO32 .....5G 13
Moor End Farm Cvn. & Camping Site
YO23: Aca M 3H 45
Moorgarth Av. YO24: York 5H 27
Moorgate YO24: York 4F 27
Moor Gro. YO24: York 1G 37
Moorland Gdns. YO23: Cop 2C 44
Moorland Gth. YO32: Stre 3H 5
Moorland Rd. YO10: York 1D 38
Moorlands Cl. YO10: Osb 3A 30
Moorlands Flds. YO10: York 1E 39
Moorlands Rd. YO30: Ske 5E 9
Moorlands Wood (Nature Reserve)
.....1F 9
Moor La. YO8: B'by 3F 57
(not continuous)
YO8: B'by, Osg 5H 57
YO19: Mur 5D 20
YO19: Nab 4B 46
YO23: Bish 1G 45
YO23: Cop 3C 44
YO23: Ruff 3H 25
YO24: Ask B, York 3C 36
YO26: Moor M 3E 15
YO26: Stut, Tad 6A 54
YO26: Up P 3H 25
YO30: Ske 5F 9
(not continuous)
YO32: Ear 2G 11
YO32: Hax 2B 4
YO32: Stre 4A 6
YO32: Wigg 5F 9
Moor Lea Av. YO24: York 6G 27
Moor Rd. YO41: Stam B 5G 23
Moorside Cvn. Pk.
YO32: Stre 2D 6
Moor Way YO32: Hunt 1G 19
Moray Cl. YO32: Stre 2C 6
Morcar Rd. YO41: Stam B 5H 23
MOREBY 2A 52
Morehall Cl. YO30: York 3H 17
Morrell Ct. YO24: York 1D 36
Morrell Gth. YO8: Sel 5D 58
Morrell Way YO10: H'tn 5G 29
Morrell Yd. YO1: York 3F 3 (3D 28)
Morritt Cl. YO31: York 4F 19
Moss Grn. Cl. YO8: Bray 5A 58
Moss Grn. La. YO8: Bray 5A 58
Moss St. YO23: York 5B 2 (4B 28)
Mossy La. YO23: Ruff 1F 35
Mount, The YO8: Sel 4C 58
YO24: York 6A 2 (5A 28)
Mount Av. YO8: Sel 4C 58
Mount Ct. YO24: York 6A 2
Mt. Ephraim
YO24: York 5A 2 (4A 28)
Mount Gro. YO8: Sel 4C 58
Mount Pde. YO24: York 6A 2 (4A 28)
Mount Pk. YO19: Ric 3B 56
MOUNT PLEASANT 5G 45
Mt. Pleasant *YO19: Ric 3B 56*
(off Main St.)
Mt. Pleasant Pk. Home Village
YO23: Aca M 6G 45
Mount Ter. YO24: York 6A 2
Mount Va. YO24: York 5A 28
Mount Va. Dr. YO24: York 5A 28
Mowbray Dr. YO26: York 3E 27
Muirfield Way YO26: York 2D 26
Mulberry Ct. YO32: Hunt 5F 11
Mulberry Dr. YO32: Hax 1D 10
Mulwith Cl. YO31: York 1G 29
Muncastergate YO31: York 6E 19
Munster Ho. *YO31: York 1C 28*
(off Townend St.)

A-Z York 67

Murray St.—Plantation Way

Murray St. YO24: York 4H **27**
Murrough Wilson Pl.
YO31: York 6C **18**
MURTON **1D 30**
Murton Gth. YO19: Mur 1D **30**
Murton La. YO19: Mur 1E **31**
Murton Way YO19: Mur, Osb 3B **30**
Museum Gdns. 2C 2 (2B 28)
Museum St. YO1: York 3D **2** (2C **28**)
Myrtle Av. YO8: Sel 4C **58**
YO23: Bish 6B **38**

N

NABURN **4B 46**
Naburn La. YO19: Dei 6G **47**
YO19: Ful 5D **38**
Naburn Lock Cvn. Pk.
YO19: Nab 5B **46**
Naburn Pk. M. YO19: Nab 3C **46**
Nairn Cl. YO24: York 3E **37**
Nalton Cl. YO23: Cop 2C **44**
Nalton St. YO8: Sel 2D **58**
Narrow La. YO32: Wigg 5A **4**
National Cen. for Early Music 4G 3
National Railway Mus. . . .2A 2 (2A 28)
Navigation Rd.
YO1: York 4G **3** (3D **28**)
Nelson's La. YO24: York 6H **27**
Nelson St. YO31: York 1D **28**
Neptune Ho. *YO10: York 4F 29*
(off Olympian Ct.)
Nessgate YO1: York 4E **3** (3C **28**)
Ness Rd. YO8: Sel 1E **59**
Nether Hornpot La. YO1: York 3E **3**
NETHER POPPLETON **3B 16**
Nether Way YO26: Up P 3B **16**
Netherwindings YO32: Hax 2F **11**
Netherwoods YO32: Stre 2A **6**
Neville Dr. YO23: Bish 6A **38**
Neville St. YO31: York 1D **28**
Neville Ter. YO31: York 1D **28**
Nevinson Gro. YO10: York 1F **39**
Nevis Way YO24: York 2D **36**
Newborough St. YO30: York 1B **28**
Newbury Av. YO24: York 6F **27**
Newby Ter. YO31: York 6C **18**
New Church Ter. YO8: Sel 2D **58**
Newcroft YO8: Sel 3C **58**
Newdale YO32: Hax 1E **11**
NEW EARSWICK **2D 18**
New Earswick Folk Hall 2D 18
New Earswick Indoor Bowls Club
. . . . .2E 19
New Earswick Nature Reserve . . .3D 18
New Earswick Sports Club 2D 18
New Forge Ct. YO32: Hax 1F **11**
Newgate YO1: York 3E **3** (3C **28**)
Newgate Mkt. YO1: York . . .3E **3** (3C **28**)
Newington Ct. YO24: York 5H **27**
Newland Pk. Cl. YO10: York 4G **29**
Newland Pk. Dr. YO10: York 4F **29**
Newlands Dr. YO26: York 1D **26**
Newlands La. YO26: Up P 5G **15**
Newlands Rd. YO23: Bish 5H **37**
New La. YO8: Sel 2D **58**
YO23: Ang 4A **34**
YO23: Bish 5A **38**
YO24: York 4G **27**
YO32: Hunt 1F **19**
YO32: Stre 2A **6**
New Millgate YO8: Sel 1D **58**
Newport Av. YO8: Sel 3C **58**
New Rd. YO19: Esc 6C **48**
YO26: Hess 6C **14**
New St. YO1: York 3D **2** (3C **28**)
YO8: Sel 2E **59**
YO26: Tad 3E **55**
Newton Ter.
YO1: York 5D **2** (4C **28**)
Newton Way YO32: Stre 5A **6**
New Wlk. YO1: York 5E **3**
YO10: York 4C **28**
New Wlk. Ter. YO10: York 5D **28**
Next Generation Club
York 4H 29
NHS WALK-IN CENTRE (YORK)
. . . . .1F 3 (2D 28)
Nicholas Gdns. YO10: York 4F **29**
Nicholas Ho. *YO10: York 4F 29*
(off Nicholas Gdns.)
Nicholas St. YO10: York 4E **29**
Nidd Cl. YO26: Neth P 5D **16**
Nidd Gro. YO24: York 1G **37**
Nigel Gro. YO24: York 5H **27**
Nightingale Cl. YO32: Hunt 4E **19**
Ninth Av. YO31: York 2F **29**
Nook, The YO8: Sel 1E **59**
Norfolk St. YO23: York 5C **28**
Norman Ct. *YO1: York 2E 3*
(off Grape La.)
Norman Dr. YO26: York 1D **26**
Normandy Cl. YO8: Sel 1C **58**
Norman St. YO10: York 4G **29**
Norseman Cl. YO19: Ric 3A **56**
Norseway YO41: Stam B 6G **23**
Nth. Back La. YO19: Whel 5C **50**
Northcote Av. YO24: York 4G **27**
Northcroft YO32: Hax 2E **11**
Nth. Eastern Ter. YO24: York 1H **37**
Northfield YO8: B'by 3F **57**
Nth. Field La. YO23: Ask B 3A **36**
YO26: Up P 1B **26**
Northfield La. YO19: Ric 2A **56**
Northfields YO32: Stre 3B **6**
Northfield Ter. YO24: York 1G **37**
Northgate La. YO41: Gate H 1E **23**
Nth. Grange Ct. YO30: York 1B **28**
Northlands Av. YO32: Ear 4F **11**
Northlands Cl. YO19: Esc 2G **53**
North La. YO19: Whel 5B **50**
YO24: York 6G **27**
YO32: Hax 2C **10**
YO32: Hunt 6F **11**
Northminster Bus. Pk.
YO26: Up P 1B **26**
North Moor YO32: Hunt 6F **11**
North Moor Cft. YO32: Hunt 6F **11**
North Moor Gdns.
YO32: Hunt 1F **19**
Nth. Moor Rd. YO32: Hunt 1F **19**
North of England Activity Cen.
. . . . .2F 25
Northolme Dr. YO30: York 4G **17**
North Pde.
YO30: York 1B **2** (2B **28**)
North St. YO1: York 3D **2** (3C **28**)
Norway Dr. YO10: York 1D **38**
Nova Scotia Way YO19: Ric 3B **56**
Nunmill St. YO23: York 5C **28**
Nunnery La. YO23: York . . .5C **2** (4B **28**)
Nunthorpe Av.
YO23: York 6C **2** (5B **28**)
Nunthorpe Cres. YO23: York 5C **28**
Nunthorpe Dr. YO23: York 5C **28**
Nunthorpe Gdns. YO23: York 5C **28**
Nunthorpe Gro. YO23: York 5B **28**
Nunthorpe Rd.
YO23: York 6C **2** (4B **28**)
Nunthorpe Vw. YO23: York 6C **28**
Nursery Ct. YO26: Neth P 3C **16**
Nursery Dr. YO24: York 4G **27**
Nursery Gdns. YO10: Osb 4A **30**
Nursery Rd. YO26: Neth P 3C **16**

O

Oak Av. YO23: Aca M 6G **45**
Oakdale Rd. YO30: York 3H **17**
Oaken Gro. YO32: Hax 1C **10**
Oak Fld. YO8: Bray 6B **58**
Oak Glade YO31: York 3F **19**
Oakhill Cres. YO32: Stre 5H **5**
Oakland Av. YO31: York 6F **19**
Oakland Dr. YO31: York 6G **19**
Oaklands YO32: Stre 4A **6**
Oaklands Sports Cen. 5E 27
Oakney Wood Dr. YO8: Sel 6E **59**
Oak Ri. YO24: York 4E **27**
Oak St. YO26: York 2G **27**
Oak Tree Cl. YO32: Stre 4A **6**
Oak Tree Ct. YO32: Hax 4C **10**
Oak Tree Gro. YO32: New E 2D **18**
Oak Tree La. YO32: Hax 4C **10**
Oak Tree Way YO32: Stre 4A **6**
Oakville St. YO31: York 6D **18**
Ogleforth YO1: York 1E **3** (2C **28**)
Ogleforth M. YO1: York 1E **3**
Old Brewery Gdns.
YO26: Tad 2F **55**
Old Coach Rd.
YO26: Heal, Tad 1E **55**
Old Coppice YO32: Hax 2F **11**
Old Dike Lands YO32: Hax 3C **10**
Old Farm Way YO8: Bray 6C **58**
Old Hall La. YO41: Kex 5G **33**
Old Highway, The
YO32: Stre 5A **6**
Oldman Ct. YO24: York 1E **37**
Old Moor La. YO24: York 2G **37**
Old Orchard YO32: Hax 3D **10**
Old Orchard, The YO10: Ful 2E **39**
YO30: Ship 1A **8**
Old Priory Ct. YO23: York 5C **2**
Old School Cl. YO10: York 3H **29**
Old School Ct. YO26: Up P 4B **16**
Old School La. YO8: B'by 4F **57**
(not continuous)
Old Village, The YO32: Hunt 1F **19**
Olympia Cres. YO8: Sel 1F **59**
Olympian Ct. YO10: York 3F **29**
Orchard, The YO10: H'tn 6G **29**
YO23: Bish 6A **38**
Orchard Cl. YO8: Sel 3B **58**
YO24: York 6G **27**
Orchard Cotts. YO19: Dun 1A **32**
Orchard Gdns. YO31: York 3E **19**
Orchard Gth. YO23: Cop 6D **36**
Orchard Paddock YO32: Hax 2D **10**
Orchard Rd. YO8: Sel 3B **58**
YO26: Up P 4B **16**
Orchard Vw. YO30: Ske 6D **8**
Orchard Way YO8: Sel 3B **58**
YO24: York 6G **27**
YO32: Stre 3A **6**
Ordnance La. YO10: York 6D **28**
Oriel Gro. YO30: York 5A **18**
Orrin Cl. YO24: York 2E **37**
OSBALDWICK **3A 30**
Osbaldwick Ind. Est.
YO19: Osb 2B **30**
Osbaldwick La.
YO10: Osb, York 3H **29**
Osbaldwick Link Rd.
YO10: Osb 3B **30**
YO19: Osb 3B **30**
Osbaldwick Village
YO10: Osb 3A **30**
Osbourne Dr. YO30: York 2G **17**
OSGODBY **5H 57**
Osmington Gdns. YO32: Stre 4H **5**
Osprey Cl. YO24: York 1D **36**
Ostler's Cl. YO23: Cop 6E **37**
Ostman Rd. YO26: York 2D **26**
Otterwood Bank YO24: York 6D **26**
Otterwood La. YO24: York 6D **26**
Otterwood Paddock
YO41: Stam B 2H **23**
OUSE ACRES **1F 27**
Ouse Acres YO26: York 2F **27**
Ouse Bank YO8: Sel 2F **59**
Ouseburn Av. YO26: York 1D **26**
Ousecliffe Gdns. YO30: York 1A **28**
Ousegate YO8: Sel 2E **59**
Ouse Lea YO30: York 6A **18**
Ouse Moor La.
YO26: Neth P 3A **16**
Ouston Cl. YO26: Tad 3F **55**
Ouston La. YO26: Tad 3F **55**
(not continuous)
Outgang YO10: H'tn 1H **39**
Outgang La. YO19: Osb 6B **20**
Outgang La. Cvn. Site
YO19: Osb 2B **30**
Overdale Cl. YO24: York 1F **37**
OVERTON **1A 16**
Overton Rd. YO30: Over 3A **8**
Ovington Ter. YO23: York 5B **28**
Owlwood Ct. YO19: Dun 2H **31**
Owlwood La. YO19: Dun 2H **31**
Owston Av. YO10: York 4G **29**
Ox Calder Cl. YO19: Dun 1A **32**
Ox Carr La. YO32: Stre 6H **5**
Ox Cl. YO41: Stam B 4H **23**
Ox Cl. La. YO10: H'tn 1C **40**
Oxford Ho. YO24: York 5A **2**
Oxford St.
YO24: York 5A **2** (4A **28**)
OXTON **3H 55**
Oxton Dr. YO26: Tad 3F **55**
Oxton La. YO26: Oxt, Tad 2E **55**

P

Paddock, The YO26: York 1E **27**
YO32: Stre 2B **6**
Paddock Cl. YO23: Ask R 4F **35**
YO23: Cop 1C **44**
YO32: Hunt 1F **19**
Paddocks, The YO19: Whel 5C **50**
Paddock Way YO26: York 1E **27**
Pagnell Av. YO8: Sel 3F **59**
Palace Vw. YO10: Ful 2D **38**
Palmer Gro. YO8: Sel 4B **58**
Palmer La. YO1: York 3G **3** (3D **28**)
Palmes Cl. YO19: Nab 3C **46**
Panman La. YO19: Holt 5B **22**
Parade Ct. YO31: York 1F **29**
Paragon Ho. YO10: York 6G **3**
Paragon St. YO10: York 6F **3** (4D **28**)
Park & Ride
Askham Bar 3G **37**
Grimston Bar 4D **30**
McArthur Glen 5D **38**
Monks Cross 4G **19**
Rawcliffe Bar 3F **17**
Park Av. YO32: New E 6D **10**
Park Cl. YO30: Ske 1D **16**
Park Cres. YO31: York 1G **3** (1D **28**)
Parker Av. YO26: York 5D **26**
Park Est. YO32: Hax 3D **10**
Park Ga. YO32: Stre 2B **6**
Park Gro. YO8: Sel 4C **58**
YO31: York 1D **28**
Parkin Av. YO8: Sel 3F **59**
Parkland Dr. YO26: Tad 2F **55**
Parkland Way YO32: Hax 3D **10**
Park La. YO24: York 4H **27**
Park Lodge YO32: New E 1E **19**
Park Row YO8: Sel 2E **59**
Parkside Cl. YO24: York 4G **27**
Parkside Commercial Cen.
YO23: York 6E **3** (5D **28**)
Park St. YO8: Sel 2E **59**
YO24: York 6B **2** (4B **28**)
Park Ter. YO32: New E 6D **10**
Parkways YO8: Sel 4C **58**
Parliament St.
YO1: York 3E **3** (3C **28**)
Parson La. YO19: Ric 3A **56**
Parsons La. YO26: Moor M 2E **15**
Paston Wlk. YO23: York 6D **2**
Pasture Cl. YO30: Ske 6D **8**
YO32: Stre 5A **6**
Pasture Farm Cl. YO10: Ful 3E **39**
Pasture La. YO31: York 5H **19**
Pastures, The YO24: York 1G **37**
Pately Pl. YO26: York 3F **27**
Patrick Pool
YO1: York 3E **3** (3C **28**)
Patrington Ho. *YO31: York 1D 28*
(off March St.)
Patterdale Dr. YO30: York 4G **17**
Pavement YO1: York 3E **3** (3C **28**)
Paver La. YO1: York 4G **3** (3D **28**)
Pear Tree Av. YO26: Up P 3B **16**
Pear Tree Cl. YO32: Hunt 1F **19**
Peartree Cl. YO8: B'by 6F **57**
Pear Tree Ct YO1: York 2F **3** (2D **28**)
Pear Tree La. YO19: Dun 2H **31**
Peasholme Grn.
YO1: York 3F **3** (3D **28**)
Peckitt St. YO1: York 5E **3** (4C **28**)
Peel Cl. YO10: H'tn 6G **29**
Peel St. YO1: York 5G **3** (4D **28**)
Pegg La. *YO26: Tad 3E 55*
(off Kirkgate)
Pelham Pl. YO32: Stre 4H **5**
Pembroke St. YO30: York 6B **18**
Penley's Ct. *YO31: York 1D 28*
(off Penley's Gro. St.)
Penley's Gro. St.
YO31: York 1F **3** (1D **28**)
Pennine Cl. YO32: Hunt 1F **19**
Penny La. Ct.
YO1: York 2F **3** (2D **28**)
Pentire Cl. YO30: York 4A **18**
Pentland Dr. YO32: Hunt 2F **19**
Penyghent Av. YO31: York 2G **29**
Peppercorn Cl. YO26: York 3G **27**
Peppercorn Ho. *YO26: York 3G 27*
(off Peppercorn Cl.)
Peppermint Way YO8: Sel 2B **58**
Percy's La. YO1: York 4G **3** (3D **28**)
Petercroft Cl. YO19: Dun 1A **32**
Petercroft La. YO19: Dun 1A **32**
Peter Hill Ct. YO30: York 5A **18**
Peter Hill Dr. YO30: York 5A **18**
Peter La. YO1: York 3E **3** (3C **28**)
Petersway YO30: York 1B **28**
Petre Av. YO8: Sel 4E **59**
Pheasant Dr. YO24: York 1D **36**
Philadelphia Ter. YO23: York 5B **28**
Phoenix Blvd.
YO26: York 2A **2** (3A **28**)
Piccadilly YO1: York 4E **3** (3C **28**)
Pickering Ho. *YO31: York 1D 28*
(off March St.)
Pike Hills Mt. YO23: Cop 6C **36**
Piker Thorn La. YO19: Mur 4E **21**
Pilgrim St. YO31: York 1C **28**
Pindars Way YO8: B'by 5F **57**
Pinelands YO32: Hax 4D **10**
Pinelands Way YO10: Osb 4A **30**
Pine Tree M. YO8: B'by 4G **57**
Pinewood Gro. YO31: York 4E **19**
Pinewood Hill YO10: York 4A **30**
Pinfold Cl. YO19: Ric 2A **56**
Pinfold Ct. YO30: York 6A **18**
Pinsent Ct. YO31: York 5E **19**
Pioneer Bus. Pk.
YO30: York 2H **17**
Pit La. YO19: Dun 2G **31**
Plantation Dr. YO8: B'by 4F **57**
YO26: York 1E **27**
Plantation Gro. YO26: York 1E **27**
Plantation Way YO32: Wigg 2C **10**

Platt La.—St Thomas's Cl.

Platt La. YO26: Up P 6H 15
Pleasant Av. YO23: Aca M 6G 45
Ploughlands YO32: Hax 3C 10
Ploughman's Cl. YO23: Cop 6E 37
Ploughmans' La. YO32: Hax 4C 10
Plumer Av. YO31: York 2G 29
Pollard Cl. YO32: Hunt 2E 19
Pond St. YO8: Sel 1E 59
Popeshead Ct. YO1: York 3E 3
Poplar Ct. YO26: York 2G 27
Poplar Farm Cvn. Pk. YO23: Aca M 3H 45
Poplar Gro. YO32: New E 2D 18
Poplars, The YO8: Bray 6A 58
Poplars Cl. YO32: Stock F 1E 21
Poplar St. YO26: York 2G 27
Poplar Tree Gdns. YO31: York 2E 29
Poppleton Hall Gdns. YO26: Neth P 2C 16
Poppleton Rd. YO24: York 3G 27
YO26: York 3G 27
Poppleton Station (Rail) 5B 16
Poppy Cl. YO8: Sel 5D 58
Portal Rd. YO26: York 1D 26
Portholme Ct. YO8: Sel 3D 58
Portholme Dr. YO8: Sel 3D 58
Portholme Rd. YO8: Sel 2D 58
Portisham Pl. YO32: Stre 4H 5
Portland St. YO31: York 1D 2 (2C 28)
Postern Cl. YO23: York . . . 6E 3 (4C 28)
Potters Dr. YO23: Cop 6D 36
Pottery La. YO31: York 6E 19
YO32: Stre 1F 5
Powell St. YO8: Sel 1C 58
Precentor's Ct. YO1: York 2D 2 (2C 28)
Prestwick Ct. YO26: York 2D 26
Price's La. YO23: York . . . 6D 2 (4C 28)
Price St. YO23: York 6C 2 (4B 28)
Priest La. YO19: Dun 6G 31
Primrose Gro. YO8: Sel 1B 58
Princess Dr. YO26: York 1F 27
Princess Rd. YO32: Stre 3A 6
Prior's Wlk. YO26: York 1F 27
Priory Ct. YO1: York 5C 2
Priory St. YO1: York 4C 2 (3B 28)
Priory Wood Way YO31: York 3F 19
Prospect Ct. YO26: Tad 2E 55
Prospect Dr. YO26: Tad 2E 55
Prospect Ho. YO1: York 5C 2
Prospect Ter. YO1: York . . 5D 2 (4C 28)
YO10: Ful 2D 38
Prospect Way YO8: Sel 3E 59
Pulleyn Cl. YO32: Stre 2C 6
Pulleyn Dr. YO24: York 6H 27
Pump Ct. *YO1: York* . . . . *3E 3* *(off Newgate)*
PUREY CUST NUFFIELD HOSPITAL 2D 2 (2C 28)
Pyramid Ct. YO26: York 1F 27

Q

Quaker Grn. YO24: York 2E 37
Quant M. YO10: York 4H 29
Quay, The YO8: Sel 1E 59
Queen Anne's Rd. YO30: York 1B 2 (2B 28)
Queens Ct. YO1: York 4D 2
Queen's Gdns. YO26: Tad 4D 54
Queen's Path, The YO1: York 2E 3 (2C 28)
Queen's Staith YO1: York 4D 2
Queen's Staith M. YO1: York 5D 2
Queen's Staith Rd. YO1: York 4D 2 (3C 28)
Queen St. YO24: York 4B 2 (3B 28)
Queenswood Gro. YO24: York . . . 5F 27
Queen Victoria St. YO23: York 6B 28

R

Racecourse Rd. YO23: York 1B 38
Radford Ho. YO24: York 6F 27
Radley Ct. YO32: Stre 5H 5
Railway Ter. YO24: York . . . . 1G 37 (Moor Gro.)
YO24: York . . . . 4A 2 (3A 28) (St Paul's Ter.)
Railway Wlk. YO30: York 2B 2 (2B 28)
Raincliffe St. YO8: Sel 2D 58
Raindale Watermill 5F 3
Rainsborough Way YO30: York 5A 18
Raker Cl. YO19: Whel 4B 50
Ramsay Cl. YO31: York 1D 28
Ramsey Av. YO23: Bish 6B 38
Ratcliffe Ct. YO30: Ske 6E 9
Ratcliffe St. YO30: York 6C 18
Raven Gro. YO26: York 3E 27
RAWCLIFFE 3G 17
Rawcliffe Av. YO30: York 5H 17
Rawcliffe Cl. YO30: York 3G 17
Rawcliffe Cft. YO30: York 3F 17
Rawcliffe Dr. YO30: York 5H 17
Rawcliffe Gro. YO30: York 6H 17
Rawcliffe Landing YO30: Ske 2E 17
Rawcliffe La. YO30: York 5H 17
Rawcliffe Way YO30: York 3G 17
Rawdon Av. YO10: York 3F 29
Raylor Cen. YO10: York 4H 3 (3E 29)
Recreation Rd. YO8: Sel 1F 59
Rectory Ct. YO1: York 5D 2
Rectory Gdns. YO23: York 6B 28
Redbarn Dr. YO10: Osb 4B 30
Redcoat Way YO24: York 1D 36
Redeness St. YO31: York 2H 3 (2E 29)
Redgrave Cl. YO31: York 5E 19
Red Ho. La. YO26: Moor M 2A 14
Red Lodge YO32: New E 2D 18
Redman Cl. YO10: York 1D 38
Redmayne Sq. YO32: Stre 2B 6
Redmires Cl. YO30: York 4A 18
Redthorn Dr. YO31: York 4F 19
Redwood Dr. YO32: Hax 2C 10
Reeves, The YO24: York 6E 27
Regen Cen. 3A 56
Regency M. YO24: York 1H 37
Regent Bldgs. *YO26: York* . . . . *3F 27* *(off York Rd.)*
Regents Ct. YO26: York 2H 27
Regents M. YO26: York 1F 27
Regent St. YO10: York 6H 3 (4E 29)
Regimental Mus., The 4E 3 (3C 28)
Reginald Gro. YO23: York 6C 28
Reginald Ter. YO8: Sel 3E 59
Reid Pk. YO32: Hax 2D 10
Reighton Av. YO30: York 5H 17
Reighton Dr. YO30: York 4H 17
Renfrew Grn. YO32: Stre 2B 6
Renshaw Gdns. YO26: York 3G 27
Reygate Gro. YO23: Cop 1D 44
Reynolds Ct. YO10: York 5H 3
Rhodes Ter. YO8: Osg 5G 57
Ribstone Gro. YO31: York 1H 29
RICCALL 3A 56
Richard III Mus. 2F 3 (2D 28)
Richardson St. YO23: York 5C 28
Richard St. YO8: Sel 2C 58
Richmond Ho. *YO10: York* . . . . *4F 29* *(off Lawrence Sq.)*
Richmond St. YO31: York 2H 3 (2E 29)
Ridgeway YO26: York 4D 26
Ridings, The YO23: Ruff 4D 24
Rievaulx Ho. *YO10: York* . . . . *4F 29* *(off Nicholas Gdns.)*
Ringstone Rd. YO30: York 2H 17
Ripley Gro. YO32: Wigg 1C 10
Ripley Ho. *YO10: York* . . . . *4F 29* *(off Lawrence Sq.)*
Risewood YO41: Gate H 2E 23
Rishworth Gro. YO30: York 3H 17
Rivelin Way YO30: York 3H 17
River Cl. YO8: B'by 3F 57
Riversdale YO32: Hax 2F 11
Riverside Cvn. & Camping Pk. YO23: Bish 5B 38
Riverside Cl. YO8: B'by 6F 57
YO41: Elv 5G 43
Riverside Cres. YO32: Hunt 5F 11
Riverside Gdns. YO26: Neth P . . . 3B 16
YO41: Elv 5G 43
Riverside Wlk. YO26: Neth P 3B 16
YO32: Stre 4H 5
River St. YO8: Sel 1E 59
YO23: York 6E 3 (4C 28)
Riversvale Dr. YO26: Neth P 3B 16
River Vw. YO8: B'by 3F 57
Robert St. YO8: Sel 2D 58
Robin Gro. YO24: York 4H 27
Robinson Ct. YO1: York 4G 3
Robinson Dr. YO24: York 5D 26
Roche Av. YO31: York 5E 19
Rockcliff Ct. YO26: Tad 2E 55
Rockingham Av. YO31: York 2G 29
Roecliffe Ct. YO26: Hess 6C 14
Rogers Ct. YO24: York 1E 37
Roland Ct. YO32: Hunt 2E 19
Rolston Av. YO31: York 3E 19
Roman Av. Nth. YO41: Stam B . . . 5G 23
Roman Av. Sth. YO41: Stam B 6G 23
Roman Bath House 3E 3
Roman Cl. YO26: Tad 2E 55
Romans Cl. YO19: Ric 3A 56
Romulus Ho. *YO10: York* . . . . *3F 29* *(off Olympian Ct.)*
Ropers Ct. YO23: Cop 6E 37
Ropewalk, The YO31: York 2H 3 (2E 29)
Roseberry Gro. YO30: York 2H 17
Rosebery St. YO26: York 1H 27
Rosebery Wood YO41: Stam B . . . 4H 23
Rosecomb Way YO32: Hax 4D 10
Rosecroft Way YO30: York 5G 17
Rosedale Av. YO26: York 4E 27
Rosedale St. YO10: York 5D 28
Rose Gth. YO8: B'by 4F 57
Rosemary Ct. YO1: York 4G 3 (3D 28)
YO26: Tad 2E 55
Rosemary Pl. YO1: York . . . 4G 3 (3D 28)
Rosemary Row YO26: Tad 2E 55
Rose St. YO31: York 6C 18
Rose Tree Gro. YO32: New E 1D 18
Rosetta Way YO26: York 1F 27
Rosslyn St. YO30: York 1A 28
Rougier St. YO24: York . . . 3C 2 (3B 28)
Rougier Ter. YO1: York . . . 4C 2 (3B 28)
Roundhill Link YO30: York 3H 17
Rowan Av. YO32: New E 2D 18
Rowan Pl. YO32: New E 1D 18
Rowley Ct. YO32: Ear 4F 11
Rowmans, The YO30: Ske 1E 17
Rowntree Av. YO30: York 5C 18
Rowntree Pk. Cvn. Pk. YO23: York 5C 28
Rowntree Wharf YO1: York 4G 3 (3D 28)
Royal Chase YO24: York 1H 37
Royal Dragoon Guards Mus., The & Regimental Association 5E 3
Royston Cl. YO32: Stre 2B 6
Ruby St. YO23: York 6B 28
Rudcarr La. YO19: Holt, W'hil . . . 4G 21
Ruddings, The YO8: Sel 3C 58
YO19: Whel 4C 50
Ruddings Cl. YO32: Hax 3C 10
Rudgate LS24: Newt K 4A 54
Rudston Ho. *YO31: York* . . . . *1D 28* *(off Penley's Gro. St.)*
Ruffhams Cl. YO19: Whel 4B 50
RUFFORTH 4D 24
Rufforth Airfield 5F 25
Runswick Av. YO26: York 3D 26
Rushwood Cl. YO32: Hax 2E 11
Russel Dr. YO30: York 5G 17
Russell St. YO23: York 5B 28
Russet Dr. YO31: York 2H 29
Rutland Cl. YO23: Cop 6C 36
Ryburn Cl. YO30: York 3H 17
Rydal Av. YO31: York 1G 29
Rye Cl. YO32: Wigg 3C 10
Ryecroft YO32: Stre 5H 5
Ryecroft Av. YO24: York 2E 37
Ryecroft Cl. YO31: York 5A 20
Ryedale Cvn. Site YO30: York 3A 18
Ryedale Ct. YO32: Hax 2D 10
Ryedale Way YO8: Sel 4D 58
Ryehill Cl. YO32: New E 6D 10
Ryemoor Rd. YO32: Hax 3C 10
Rylatt Pl. YO26: York 4D 26

S

Sadberge Ct. YO10: York 4A 30
Saddlebrook Ct. YO24: York 1F 37
Saddlers Cl. YO23: Cop 6D 36
YO32: Hunt 3F 19
Saddlers Wlk. YO19: Esc 3F 53
Sails Dr. YO10: York 4H 29
St Aelreds Cl. YO31: York 3F 29
St Aidans Wlk. YO26: Stut 6C 54
St Andrewgate YO1: York 3E 3 (3C 28)
St Andrew Pl. YO1: York 3F 3 (3D 28)
St Andrew's Ct. YO1: York 3F 3
St Ann's Ct. YO10: York 6G 3 (5E 29)
St Aubyn's Pl. YO24: York 5A 28
St Barnabas Cl. YO26: York 2H 27
St Benedict Rd. YO23: York 6D 2 (4C 28)
St Bridget Ct. YO23: York 6E 3
St Catherines Cl. YO30: Ske 6E 9
YO41: Stam B . . . . *4H 23* *(off Moor Rd.)*
St Catherine's Ct. YO24: York 6A 2 (4A 28)
St Catherine's Pl. YO24: York 6A 2
St Chads Wharf YO23: York 1C 38
St Clement's Gro. YO23: York 5C 28
St Denys Ct. YO1: York 4G 3
St Denys' Rd. YO1: York . . . 4F 3 (3D 28)
St Edmunds YO41: Stam B 4G 23
St Edward's Cl. YO24: York 1H 37
St George's Fld. YO10: York 5F 3
St George's Pl. YO24: York 5H 27
St Giles Ct. YO30: York 1D 2 (2C 28)
St Giles Ga. YO30: York 1D 2
St Giles Rd. YO30: Ske 6D 8
St Giles Way YO23: Cop 1C 44
St Gregorys M. YO1: York 4C 2 (3B 28)
St Helen's Ri. YO19: Whel 5C 50
St Helen's Rd. YO24: York 1G 37
St Helen's Sq. YO1: York 3D 2 (3C 28)
St Hilda's M. YO10: York 3H 29
St James Cl. YO30: York 2G 17
St James Ct. YO26: York 2A 28
St James Mt. YO23: York 5A 28
St James Pl. YO24: York 6F 27
St James Ter. YO8: Sel 2D 58
St John M. YO8: Sel 1C 58
St John's Cres. YO31: York 1F 3 (1D 28)
St John's Rd. YO41: Stam B 4H 23
St Johns Sq. *YO8: Sel* . . . . *2D 58* *(off New La.)*
St John's St. YO31: York 1E 3 (2C 28)
St John's Wlk. YO41: Stam B 5H 23
St Josephs Ct. YO24: York 6D 26
St Joseph's St. YO26: Tad 3D 54
St Lawrence Ct. YO10: H'tn 6H 29
St Leonards Av. YO8: Osg 5G 57
ST LEONARD'S HOSPICE 3G 37
St Leonard's Pl. YO1: York 2D 2 (2C 28)
St Luke's Gro. YO30: York 6B 18
St Margaret's Ter. YO1: York 4G 3 (3E 29)
St Mark's Gro. YO30: York 3G 17
St Marks Sq. *YO8: Sel* . . . . *2D 58* *(off New La.)*
St Martin's La. YO1: York 4C 2 (3B 28)
St Mary's YO30: York 1C 2 (2B 28)
St Mary's Abbey (remains of) 2C 2
St Mary's Cl. YO32: Stre 3A 6
YO32: Wigg 2C 10
St Mary's Ct. YO24: York 5B 2 (4B 28)
St Mary's Gro. YO10: Osb 3A 30
St Mary's La. YO30: York 1C 2 (2B 28)
St Mary's M. YO32: Wigg 1C 10
St Mary's Sq. YO1: York 4F 3
St Marys Ter. YO30: York 2C 2
St Marys Vw. YO8: Sel 5C 58
St Matthew's Cl. YO19: Nab 4B 46
St Matthew's Ct. YO19: Nab 4B 46
St Maurice Ct. YO31: York 1F 3
St Maurice's Rd. YO31: York 1F 3 (2D 28)
St Michaels Ct. YO41: Sutt D 6H 43
St Nicholas Av. YO19: Ful 5D 38
St Nicholas Cl. YO23: Cop 6C 36
St Nicholas Cres. YO23: Cop 6C 36
St Nicholas Cft. YO23: Ask B 4H 35
St Nicholas Pl. YO10: York 4F 29
St Nicholas Rd. YO23: Cop 6C 36
St Nicholas Way YO32: Wigg 2C 10
St Olave's Rd. YO30: York 1B 28
St Oswalds Ct. YO10: Ful 3D 38
St Oswald's Rd. YO10: York 1C 38
St Paul's M. YO24: York 4A 2 (4A 28)
St Paul's Sq. YO24: York 4A 28
St Paul's Ter. YO24: York 5A 2 (4A 28)
St Peters Cl. YO26: Knap 2C 26
St Peters Ct. YO30: York 1B 28
St Peter's Gro. YO30: York 1B 28
St Philip's Gro. YO30: York 5A 18
St Sampson's Sq. YO1: York 3E 3 (3C 28)
St Saviourgate YO1: York 3F 3 (3D 28)
St Saviour's Pl. YO1: York 3F 3 (3D 28)
St Stephens M. YO26: York 4E 27
St Stephen's Rd. YO24: York 5E 27
St Stephen's Sq. YO24: York 6E 27
St Swithin's Wlk. YO26: York 3G 27
St Thomas' Pl. YO31: York 1C 28
St Thomas's Cl. YO10: Osb 3A 30

A-Z York 69

St Vincent Row—Temple La.

St Vincent Row YO41: Sutt D 1H 51
St Vincent's Cl. YO41: Sutt D 6H 43
St Wilfrid's Cl. YO8: Bray 5A 58
YO32: Stre 6A 6
St Wilfrid's Ct. YO8: Bray 6A 58
YO31: York 1F 3
St Wilfrid's Cres. YO8: Bray 6A 58
St Wilfrid's Rd. YO32: Stre 5A 6
St Williams College 2E 3
St Wulstan Cl. YO31: York 6E 19
Salisbury Rd. YO26: York 2H 27
Salisbury Ter. YO26: York 2H 27
Salmond Rd. YO24: York 6D 26
Sandacre Ct. YO26: York 2F 27
Sandcroft Cl. YO24: York 1F 37
Sandcroft Rd. YO24: York 1F 37
Sanderson Ct. YO26: York 4D 26
Sandfield Ter. YO26: Tad 2F 55
Sandhill La. YO8: Sel 3A 58
YO41: Sutt D 6H 43
Sand Hole La. YO30: Ship 2B 8
Sandholme YO32: Hax 1E 11
Sandiacres YO8: Bray 5A 58
Sand La. YO8: B'by 1F 57
YO8: Osg 5H 57
Sandmartin Ct. YO24: York 1F 37
Sandown Cl. YO24: York 5F 27
Sandringham Cl. YO32: Hax 4C 10
Sandringham St. YO10: York 5D 28
Sandstock Rd. YO31: York 6H 19
Sandy Gap YO32: Hax 4C 10
Sandyland YO32: Hax 2C 10
Sandy La. YO32: Hax 2C 10
YO32: Stock F 6F 13
Sandyridge YO26: Neth P 4C 16
Sandy Ri. YO8: Sel 4D 58
Sargent Av. YO23: Bish 5H 37
Saturn Ho. *YO10: York 3F 29*
(off Olympian Ct.)
Saunter's Way YO19: Ric 3A 56
Saville Gro. YO30: York 5A 18
Sawyer's Cres. YO23: Cop 6D 36
Sawyers Wlk. YO19: Dun 1A 32
Saxford Way YO32: Wigg 1B 10
Saxon Cl. YO30: Ship 2A 8
Saxon Pl. YO31: York 6E 19
Saxon Rd. YO41: Stam B 5G 23
Saxon Va. YO30: Ship 2B 8
Scafell Cl. YO30: York 4G 17
Scagglethorpe La.
YO26: Moor M 1E 15
Scaife Gdns. YO31: York 6D 18
Scaife St. YO31: York 6C 18
Scarborough Ter. YO30: York 1C 28
SCARCROFT 6B 2 (5B 28)
Scarcroft Ct. YO8: Bray 5B 58
Scarcroft Hill
YO24: York 6B 2 (5B 28)
Scarcroft La.
YO23: York 6C 2 (4B 28)
Scarcroft Rd.
YO23: York 6B 2 (4B 28)
YO24: York 6B 2 (4B 28)
Scarcroft Vw.
YO23: York 6C 2 (4B 28)
Scaudercroft YO19: Dun 1A 32
Scawton Av. YO31: York 3E 19
School Cl. YO8: Sel 4C 58
YO30: Ske 6E 9
YO41: Stam B 5G 23
School La. YO10: Ful 2E 39
YO10: H'tn 6H 29
YO23: Bish 5A 38
YO23: Cop 1C 44
YO26: Up P 4A 16
School St. YO24: York 4F 27
SCOREBY 2F 23
Scoreby La. YO41: Gate H 3F 23
Scott Moncrieff Rd. YO32: Stre 6A 6
Scott Rd. YO8: Sel 1D 58
Scott St. YO23: York 5C 28
Scriven Gro. YO32: Hax 2E 11
Scrope Av.
YO31: York 1H 3 (2E 29)
Seafire Cl. YO30: York 2B 18
Seakel La. YO23: Ang 4D 34
Seaton Cl. YO10: York 3A 30
Second Av. YO31: York 1F 29
Sedge Ri. YO26: Tad 4C 54
Sefton Av. YO31: York 5F 19
Segrave Wlk. YO26: York 3G 27
SELBY 2E 59
Selby Abbey 2E 59
Selby Bus. Pk. YO8: Sel 6E 59
Selby Ho. *YO31: York 1C 28*
(off Townend St.)
Selby Indoor Bowling Club 5C 58
Selby Rd. YO19: Ful 3E 39
YO19: Ric 4C 56
Selby Station (Rail) 2E 59
SELBY WAR MEMORIAL HOSPITAL
. . . . 3C 58
Seldon Rd. YO26: York 2G 27
Settle Ho. *YO26: York 3G 27*
(off Burnsall Dr.)
Seventh Av. YO31: York 2F 29
Severn Grn. YO26: Neth P 5E 17
Severus Av. YO24: York 3F 27
Severus St. YO24: York 4F 27
Seymour Gro. YO31: York 1F 29
Shallowdale Gro. YO10: Osb 3A 30
Shambles YO1: York 3E 3 (3C 28)
Shaw's Ter. YO24: York 5B 2 (4B 28)
Shelley Dr. YO32: Stre 4H 5
Shelley Gro. YO30: York 4H 17
Shelley Ho. YO26: York 3F 27
Sherbourne Gro. YO32: Stre 4A 6
Sheriff Hutton Rd. YO32: Stre 1A 6
Sherringham Dr. YO24: York 1F 37
Sherwood Gro. YO26: York 2D 26
YO31: York 4F 19
Shilton Gth. Cl. YO32: Ear 4F 11
SHIPTON 1A 8
Shipton La. YO32: Wigg 1C 8
Shipton Rd. YO30: Ske, York 5D 8
Shipton St. YO30: York 6B 18
Shipyard Rd. YO8: Sel 2F 59
Shirbutt La. YO26: Hess 6C 14
Shireburn Gro. YO8: Sel 4E 59
Shirley Av. YO26: York 1E 27
Shopping Precinct, The
YO23: Cop 1D 44
Shotel Cl. YO30: York 5H 17
Siding La. YO8: B'by 4F 57
Sidings, The YO32: Stre 3B 6
Silverdale Ct. YO24: York 2F 37
Silver St. YO1: York 3E 3 (3C 28)
YO19: Ric 3A 56
Sim Balk La. YO23: Bish, York . . . 4G 37
Simmons Cl. YO32: Stre 4H 5
Sinnington Ho. *YO31: York 1D 28*
(off Lowther St.)
Sir Jack Lyons Concert Hall 5G 29
Sir John Hunt Memorial Homes
YO10: York 1D 38
Sirocco Ct. YO31: York 5E 19
Sitwell Gro. YO26: York 2E 27
Siward St. YO10: York 4G 29
Siwards Way YO10: H'tn 5G 29
Sixth Av. YO31: York 2F 29
Skeldergate YO1: York 4D 2 (3C 28)
SKELTON 6E 9
Skelton Ct. YO30: York 1A 28
Skewsby Gro. YO31: York 4F 19
Skiddaw YO24: York 2E 37
Skipton Ho. *YO10: York 4F 29*
(off Lawrence Sq.)
Skipwith Rd. YO19: Esc 2F 53
Slaidburn Ho. *YO26: York 3G 27*
(off Burnsall Dr.)
Slessor Rd. YO24: York 6D 26
Slice La. YO26: Oxt 3H 55
Slingsby Gro. YO24: York 1G 37
Smales' St. YO1: York 5D 2 (4C 28)
Smary La. YO19: Mur 1E 31
Smeaton Gro. YO26: York 2E 27
Smith Cl. YO10: York 1F 39
Smithie Cl. YO32: New E 6D 10
Snowdon Cl. YO23: Ask R 4F 35
Somerset Cl. YO30: York 2G 17
Somerset Rd. YO31: York 5D 18
SOUTH BANK 6B 28
Sth. Bank Av. YO23: York 6B 28
Sth. Down Rd. YO32: Hunt 6F 11
Sth. Duffield Rd. YO8: Osg 5H 57
(not continuous)
South Esplanade
YO1: York 5E 3 (4C 28)
Southfield Cl. YO23: Ruff 4E 25
Southfield Cres. YO24: York 1G 37
Southfields Rd. YO32: Stre 3A 6
South Gth. YO30: Ship 2A 8
Southlands YO32: Hax 1C 10
Southlands Cl. YO19: Esc 2G 53
Southlands Rd. YO23: York 5B 28
South La. YO32: Hax 2C 10
Southolme Dr. YO30: York 5H 17
South Pde.
YO23: York 5B 2 (4B 28)
Sth. Rudding La. YO19: Whel 6B 50
South Vw. YO8: Osg 5H 57
South Vw. Ter. YO24: York 4E 27
Sowerby Rd. YO26: York 3F 27
Spalding Av. YO30: York 6A 18
Speculation St.
YO1: York 4H 3 (3E 29)
Spencer St. YO23: York . . . 6D 2 (4C 28)
Speng La. YO26: Hut W 2A 34
Spen La. YO1: York 2F 3 (2D 28)
Spey Bank YO24: York 3E 37
Spindle Cl. YO24: York 1E 37
Spinney, The YO24: York 2H 37
Springbank Av. YO19: Dun 1H 31
Springfield Cl. YO8: B'by 4G 57
YO31: York 6H 19
Springfield Ct. YO24: York 4H 27
Springfield Dr. YO8: B'by 4F 57
Springfield Rd. YO26: Up P 3B 16
Springfield Way YO31: York 6H 19
Spring Hill YO26: Tad 2E 55
Springhill Ct. YO26: Tad 2E 55
Spring La. YO10: H'tn 5G 29
(not continuous)
YO26: Hut W 6A 24
Spring Wlk. YO8: Bray 6B 58
Springwood YO32: Hax 4D 10
Springwood Gro. YO26: York 1E 27
Spruce Cl. YO32: New E 3D 18
Spurr Ct. YO24: York 1E 37
Spurriergate
YO1: York 3E 3 (3C 28)
Spurriergate Cen. *YO1: York 3C 28*
(off Spurriergate)
Spurriergate Ho. YO1: York 4E 3
Square, The YO26: Tad 2F 55
YO41: Stam B 4G 23
Stabler Cl. YO32: Wigg 2A 10
Stablers Wlk. YO32: Ear 4F 11
Stafford Ho. YO24: York 5A 2
Staindale Cl. YO30: York 3G 17
Staithes Cl. YO26: York 3D 26
Stakers Orchard YO23: Cop 1D 44
STAMFORD BRIDGE 5G 23
Stamford Bridge Battle Site (1066)
. . . . 5H 23
Stamford Bri. Rd.
YO19: Dun, Mur 3E 31
Stamford Bri. W. YO41: Stam B . . . 1H 23
Stamford St. E. YO26: York 2H 27
Stamford St. W. YO26: York 2H 27
Staniland Dr. YO8: Sel 2B 58
Stanley Av. YO32: Hax 5D 10
Stanley St. YO31: York 6D 18
Starkey Cres. YO31: York 2G 29
Station Av. YO24: York 3C 2 (3B 28)
YO32: New E 2D 18
Station Bus. Pk. YO26: York 3H 27
Station Cl. YO19: Ric 3B 56
Station Ind. Est. YO26: Tad 3D 54
Station La. YO30: Ship 1A 8
Station Ri. YO1: York 3C 2 (3B 28)
YO24: York 3C 2 (3B 28)
Station Rd. YO8: Sel 2E 59
YO19: Ric 3B 56
YO23: Cop 1C 44
YO24: York 4B 2 (3B 28)
YO26: Tad 3C 54
YO26: Up P 4B 16
YO32: Hax 2D 10
Station Sq. YO32: Stre 4A 6
Staynor Av. YO8: Sel 4F 59
Steadings Yd. YO32: Stre 2C 6
Steeple Cl. YO32: Wigg 1B 10
Stephenson Cl. YO32: Hunt 4E 19
Stephenson Way YO26: York 2H 27
Stephen's Wlk. YO8: Bray 6C 58
Sterne Av. YO31: York 2G 29
Steward Cl. YO8: Bray 6A 58
Stillingfleet Rd.
YO19: Esc, Still 5B 52
Stirling Gro. YO10: York 1F 39
Stirling Rd. YO30: York 2H 17
Stirrup Cl. YO24: York 1D 36
Stockhill Cl. YO19: Dun 1H 31
Stockholm Cl. YO10: York 6D 28
STOCKTON HALL HOSPITAL 1E 21
Stockton La. YO31: York 1F 29
YO32: Stock F, York 3C 20
STOCKTON-ON-THE FOREST
. . . . 1F 21
Stonebow, The
YO1: York 3F 3 (3D 28)
Stonegate YO1: York 2D 2 (2C 28)
Stonegate Ct. YO1: York 2D 2
Stonelands Ct. YO30: York 4A 18
Stone Riggs YO32: Stock F 1F 21
Stones Cl. YO24: York 5G 27
Stonethwaite YO24: York 2E 37
Stonewall Cott. La.
YO41: Stam B 5G 23
Stoop Cl. YO32: Wigg 3C 10
Stow Ct. YO32: Hunt 2E 19
Straight La. YO19: Holt 4A 22
Straker's Pas. *YO1: York 3F 3*
(off Fossgate)
Strand Ho. YO1: York 5F 3
Stratford Way YO32: Hunt 2E 19
Stray Gth. YO31: York 6F 19
Straylands Gro. YO31: York 5F 19
Stray Rd. YO31: York 1H 29
STRENSALL 3A 6
STRENSALL CAMP 6A 6
Strensall Pk. YO32: Stre 1H 11
Strensall Rd.
YO32: Ear, Hunt, Stre 6F 11
Stripe La. YO30: Ske 6C 8
Stuart Cl. YO32: Stre 2C 6
Stuart Rd. YO24: York 6F 27
Stubden Gro. YO30: York 3H 17
Sturdee Gro. YO31: York 6E 19
STUTTON 6C 54
Stutton Rd. YO26: Stut, Tad 6C 54
Suffolk Ho. YO24: York 5A 2
Summerfield Rd. YO24: York 2E 37
Summer Gdns. YO30: York 5H 17
Summerhouse M.
YO30: York 1C 2 (2B 28)
Sunningdale Cl. YO26: York 2D 26
Sunnydale YO32: Hax 4D 10
Surrey Way YO30: York 5H 17
Surtees St. YO30: York 6B 18
Susan Ct.
YO31: York 1H 3 (1E 29)
Susscarrs La. YO19: Whel 6D 50
Sussex Cl. YO10: York 5A 30
Sussex Rd. YO10: York 5A 30
Sussex Way YO32: Stre 4H 5
Sutherland St. YO23: York 6B 28
Sutor Cl. YO23: Cop 6D 36
Sutton Pk. YO41: Sutt D 6H 43
Sutton Rd. YO32: Wigg 4A 4
SUTTON UPON DERWENT 6H 43
Sutton Way YO30: York 5B 18
Swale Av. YO24: York 1G 37
Swallow Hall Leisure Complex
. . . . 2F 49
Swan Cl. YO19: Dei 6H 47
Swan Farm Ct. YO19: Dei 6H 47
Swann St. YO23: York 6C 2 (4B 28)
Swarthdale YO32: Hax 1E 11
Swinegate
YO1: York 3E 3 (3C 28)
Swinegate Ct. E. YO1: York 2E 3
Swinegate Ct. W. YO1: York 2E 3
Swinerton Av. YO26: York 1H 27
Swinsty Ct. YO30: York 4H 17
Swinton Cl. YO30: York 3G 17
Sycamore Av. YO32: New E 1D 18
Sycamore Cl. YO8: Sel 3B 58
YO30: Ske 6E 9
YO32: Hax 4D 10
Sycamore Ct. YO8: B'by 3F 57
YO32: New E 1E 19
(off Sycamore Pl.)
Sycamore Pl.
YO30: York 1B 2 (2B 28)
YO32: New E 1E 19
Sycamore Rd. YO8: B'by 3F 57
Sycamore Ter.
YO30: York 2B 2 (2B 28)
Sycamore Vw. YO26: Up P 4B 16
Sykes Cl. YO19: Whel 5C 50
YO30: York 1B 28
(off St Olave's Rd.)

T

TADCASTER 4C 54
Tadcaster Community Swimming Pool
. . . . 2D 54
Tadcaster Leisure Cen. 3D 54
Tadcaster Rd. YO23: York 6C 36
YO24: York 4G 37
(not continuous)
Talbot Ct. YO1: York 2E 3
Talbot Ho. YO24: York 5A 2
Tamworth Rd. YO30: York 4A 18
TANG HALL 3G 29
Tang Hall La. YO10: York 2F 29
YO31: York 2F 29
Tanner Row YO1: York 4C 2 (3B 28)
Tanner's Moat
YO1: York 3C 2 (3B 28)
Tanner St. YO1: York 3C 2 (3C 28)
Tannery, The YO10: York 5H 3 (4E 29)
Tannery M. YO10: York 5H 3 (4E 29)
Tarbert Cres. YO24: York 2D 36
Tatton Cl. YO30: York 4B 18
Taylors Cl. YO19: Holt 4A 22
Teal Dr. YO24: York 1E 37
Tea Room Sq. *YO24: York 3B 2*
(off Station Rd.)
Teck St. YO23: York 6E 3 (5C 28)
Tedder Rd. YO24: York 6D 26
Telford Ter. YO24: York 5B 28
Templar Way YO8: Sel 5D 58
Temple Av. YO10: York 3H 29
Temple Gth. YO23: Cop 2E 45
Temple La. YO23: Aca M, Cop 1D 44

Templemead—White Rose Gro.

Templemead YO31: York 5E **19**
Temple Rd. YO23: Bish 5H **37**
Temple Wlk. YO19: Esc 5G **53**
Tennant St. YO8: Sel 1C **58**
Tennent Rd. YO24: York 5D **26**
Tennyson Av. YO30: York 6C **18**
Ten Thorn La. YO26: Knap 3C **26**
Terrace, The YO23: Ruff 4E **25**
Terrington Cl. YO32: Stre 2A **6**
Terry Av. YO23: York 5E **3** (4C **28**)
Terry St. YO23: York 6C **28**
Thames Ho. YO10: York 5G **3**
Thanet Rd. YO24: York 6F **27**
Thatch Cl. YO8: Sel 3D **58**
Thatchers Cft. YO23: Cop 6D **36**
The ....
Names prefixed with 'The'
for example 'The Approach'
are indexed under the main name
such as 'Approach, The'
Theakstone Ct. YO30: Ship 1A **8**
Theatre Royal 2D 2 (2C 28)
Theresa Cl. YO32: Hunt 4F **19**
Thief La. YO8: B'lw 6E **59**
YO10: York 4F **29**
YO26: Hess 1F **25**
Third Av. YO31: York 2F **29**
Thirkleby Way YO10: Osb 3A **30**
(not continuous)
Thirlmere Dr. YO31: York 1G **29**
Thirsk Ho. *YO31: York* *1C 28*
(off Backhouse St.)
Thistle Cl. YO8: Sel 5D **58**
Thistleton Ct. YO10: York 4G **3**
Thomas St. YO8: Sel 1E **59**
YO10: York 5H **3** (4E **29**)
Thompson Cl. YO8: Osg 5G **57**
Thompson Dr. YO32: Stre 2C **6**
Thompson Pl. YO26: York 2G **27**
Thoresby Rd. YO24: York 6D **26**
Thornaby Ho. *YO31: York* *1C 28*
(off Townend St.)
Thornbeck YO19: Dun 3H **31**
Thorncroft YO19: Dun 1A **32**
Thornden Bldgs. YO8: Sel 2E **59**
Thornfield Av. YO31: York 5F **19**
Thornfield Dr. YO31: York 3E **19**
Thornhills YO32: Hax 2F **11**
Thorn Nook YO31: York 5F **19**
Thornton Moor Cl. YO30: York 3H **17**
Thorntree Gro. YO30: York 3B **18**
Thornwood Covert
YO24: York 6E **27**
Thorpe St. YO23: York 5B **28**
Three Lakes Retail Pk.
YO8: Sel 4E **59**
Thurston Ho. YO23: York 6E **3**
Tilmire Cl. YO10: York 1F **39**
Tinker La. YO23: Ruff 3F **25**
Tisbury Rd. YO26: York 3G **27**
Tithe Cl. YO24: York 6D **26**
Toby Ct. YO32: Stre 4A **6**
Toft Grn. YO1: York 4B **2** (3B **28**)
Toll Bar Way YO26: Tad 1G **55**
Topcliffe Ct. YO8: Sel 1C **58**
Top La. YO23: Cop 6C **36**
Toremill Cl. YO32: New E 1D **18**
Torridon Pl. YO24: York 2D **36**
Tostig Av. YO26: York 2E **27**
Tostig Cl. YO41: Stam B 5G **23**
Tourist Info. Cen.
Selby 1E 59
York, St Leonard's Pl.
...............2D 2 (2C 28)
York Station 4B 2 (3B 28)
Tower Ct. YO30: York 3A **18**
Tower Cres. YO26: Tad 2C **54**
Tower Pl. YO1: York 5E **3**
Tower St. YO1: York 5E **3** (4C **28**)
Town End Gdns. YO32: Wigg 1B **10**
Townend St. YO31: York 1C **28**
TOWTHORPE 1G **11**
Towthorpe Moor La.
YO32: Stock F, Tow 1H **11**
Towthorpe Rd. YO32: Hax, Tow ...2E **11**
Towton Av. YO24: York 5H **27**
Tradewinds *YO10: York* *4F 29*
(off Lawrence St.)
Trafalgar Ho. YO1: York 5F **3**
Trafalgar St. YO23: York 6B **28**
Tranby Av. YO10: Osb 3B **30**
Treasurer's House 2C 28
Trenchard Rd. YO26: York 1D **26**
Trenfield Ct. YO24: York 4H **27**
Trent Av. YO32: Hunt 5G **11**
Trentholme Dr. YO24: York 5A **28**
Trentholme Ho. YO24: York 5A **28**
Trent Ho. YO10: York 5G **3**
Trent Way YO24: York 2F **37**
Trevor Gro. YO24: York 5H **27**
Tribune Way YO30: York 3B **18**
Trinity Ct.
YO1: York 4C **2** (3B **28**)
Trinity La. YO1: York 4C **2** (3B **28**)
Trinity Mdws. YO32: Stock F 1F **21**
Troon Cl. YO26: York 2D **26**
Troutbeck YO24: York 2E **37**
Troutsdale Av. YO30: York 3G **17**
Tudor Croft *2D 30*
(off Murton La.)
Tudor Rd. YO24: York 5E **27**
Tudor Way YO32: Stre 2C **6**
Tuke Av. YO10: York 3H **29**
Tuke Ho. YO1: York 5D **2**
Tune St. YO8: Osg 5G **57**
Turbary La. YO32: Hunt 5B **12**
Turks Head Ct. YO1: York 2E **3**
Turnberry Dr. YO26: York 3D **26**
Turner's Cft. YO10: H'tn 6G **29**
Turner's Sq. *YO8: Sel* *2D 58*
(off Gowthorpe)
Turnhead Ct. YO8: B'by 2F **57**
Turnhead Cres. YO8: B'by 3F **57**
Turnmire Rd. YO24: York 1G **37**
Turnpike Rd. YO26: Tad 1G **55**
Turpin Ct. YO1: York 5F **3**
Turton Sq. YO8: Bray 6C **58**
Twinam Ct. YO19: Dun 1B **32**
Twin Pike Way YO32: Wigg 2B **10**
Tyburn Ct. YO24: York 5A **28**
Tyneham Way YO32: Stre 4A **6**
Tyn Garth YO23: Aca M 4H **45**

U

Ullswater YO24: York 2E **37**
Undercroft YO19: Dun 1A **32**
Union La. YO8: Sel 3D **58**
Union Ter. YO31: York 1C **28**
University of York, The
Heslington 6G 29
Sally Baldwin Buildings *5G 29*
(off Wentworth Way)
The King's Manor ...2D 2 (2B 28)
University of York Sports Cen., The
.......................6F 29
University Rd.
YO10: H'tn, York 5F **29**
Uppercroft YO32: Hax 3C **10**
Up. Hanover St. YO26: York 2H **27**
Up. Newborough St.
YO30: York 6C **18**
UPPER POPPLETON 4B **16**
Up. Price St. YO23: York ...6C **2** (5B **28**)
Up. St Paul's Ter. YO24: York 3A **28**
Usher La. YO32: Hax 2E **11**
Usher Pk. Rd. YO32: Hax 1E **11**

V

Vale, The YO30: Ske 6D **8**
Valley Vw. YO19: Whel 5B **50**
Vanbrugh Dr. YO10: York 4A **30**
Vanbrugh Way YO10: H'tn 5G **29**
Vavasour Ct. YO23: Cop 1D **44**
Vengeance La. YO19: Dun 1F **31**
Vernon Cl. YO23: Bish 6A **38**
Vernon Rd. YO30: York 3G **17**
Vesper Dr. YO24: York 4D **26**
Vesper Wlk. YO32: Hunt 5F **11**
Vesta Ho. *YO10: York* *3F 29*
(off Olympian Ct.)
Viaduct Wlk. YO26: Tad 2D **54**
Vicarage Gdns. YO10: Osb 3A **30**
Vicarage La. YO19: Nab 4B **46**
Vicars Cl. YO23: Cop 1D **44**
Victoria Bar Apartments
YO1: York 5D **2**
Victoria Ct. YO26: York 2H **27**
Victoria Farm Cl. YO23: Ruff 4D **24**
Victoria Farm Est. YO30: York 4A **18**
Victoria St. YO23: York 6D **2** (4C **28**)
Victoria Way YO32: Hunt 4E **19**
Victor St. YO1: York 5D **2** (4C **28**)
Viking Cl. YO41: Stam B 5G **23**
Viking Dr. YO19: Ric 3A **56**
Viking Rd. YO26: York 2E **27**
YO41: Stam B 5G **23**
Villa Ct. YO26: York 6D **16**
Village, The YO30: Ske 5D **8**
YO32: Hax, Wigg 2B **10**
YO32: Stock F 1E **21**
YO32: Stre 3A **6**
Village Gth. YO32: Wigg 1C **10**
Village St. YO30: York 2G **17**
Villa Gro. YO31: York 1E **29**
Vincent Way YO24: York 1E **37**
Vine St. YO23: York 6D **2** (5C **28**)
Vivars Cen., The YO8: Sel 2E **59**
Vivars Way YO8: Sel 2E **59**
Volta St. YO8: Sel 3F **59**
Vue Cinema
York 2H 17
Vulcan Ho. *YO10: York* *3F 29*
(off Olympian Ct.)
Vyner Ho. YO24: York 4E **27**
Vyner St. YO31: York 6C **18**

W

Waggoners Dr. YO23: Cop 6D **36**
Wain Cl. YO32: Hunt 6F **11**
Waincroft YO32: Stre 5H **5**
Wainers Cl. YO23: Cop 6D **36**
Wain's Gro. YO24: York 2F **37**
Wain's Rd. YO24: York 1F **37**
Walker Dr. YO24: York 1D **36**
Walker La. YO19: Whel 5B **50**
Walled Garden, The
YO19: Nab 4B **46**
Walmer Carr YO32: Wigg 2A **10**
WALMERGATE STRAY 6F **29**
Walmgate
YO1: York 4F **3** (3D **28**)
YO10: York 4D **28**
Walmgate Bar 5H 3 (4D 28)
Walney Rd. YO31: York 2G **29**
Walnut Cl. YO10: H'tn 6G **29**
YO32: Hax 2D **10**
Walpole St. YO31: York 6D **18**
Waltham Cl. YO32: Stre 2C **6**
Walton Pl. YO26: York 4D **26**
Walworth St. Nth. YO26: York 2H **27**
Walworth St. W. YO26: York 2H **27**
Wandhill YO32: Hax 2C **10**
Wandle, The YO26: York 5C **26**
Wansbeck YO24: York 2D **36**
Ward Ct. YO23: York 6D **2**
WARTHILL 2B **22**
Warwick St. YO31: York 6D **18**
Wasdale Cl. YO30: York 4G **17**
Waterdale Pk. YO31: York 4E **19**
Water End YO26: York 2G **27**
YO30: York 2G **27**
Waterfront YO8: Sel 2F **59**
Water Hill La. YO8: Sel 2E **59**
Waterings YO32: Wigg 2B **10**
Water La. YO8: Sel 1E **59**
YO19: Dun 1A **32**
YO30: York 6A **18**
Waterman Ct. YO24: York 6D **26**
Waterside Gdns. YO31: York 5D **18**
Waterworld 3G 19
Watson St. YO24: York 5A **2** (4A **28**)
Watson Ter. YO24: York ...5A **2** (4A **28**)
Wattlers Cl. YO23: Cop 6E **37**
Wavell St. YO8: Sel 1B **58**
Waveney Gro. YO30: York 5B **18**
Waverley St. YO31: York ...1F **3** (2D **28**)
Waynefleet Gro. YO10: York 4G **29**
Weavers Cl. YO23: Cop 6D **36**
Weavers Pk. YO23: Cop 6D **36**
Weddall Cl. YO24: York 6H **27**
Weedling Ga. YO26: Stut 6C **54**
Weir Cvn. Site YO41: Stam B 4G **23**
Welborn Cl. YO10: York 3G **29**
Welland Ri. YO26: York 2F **27**
Wellesley Cl. YO30: York 3A **18**
Well Gth. YO10: H'tn 6H **29**
Wellington Row
YO1: York 3D **2** (3C **28**)
Wellington St.
YO10: York 6H **3** (4E **29**)
Wells Cl. YO8: Sel 2B **58**
Welton Av. YO26: York 2F **27**
Welwyn Dr. YO10: York 1E **39**
Wenham Rd. YO24: York 1E **37**
Wenlock Dr. YO19: Esc 2G **53**
Wenlock Gdns. YO19: Whel 4C **50**
Wenlock Ter. YO10: York 6D **28**
Wensleydale Dr. YO10: Osb 3B **30**
Wensley Ho. *YO26: York* *3G 27*
(off Bouthwaite Dr.)
Wentworth Rd. YO24: York 5B **28**
Wentworth Way YO10: H'tn 5G **29**
Werkdyke, The YO1: York 2F **3**
Wesley Pl. YO1: York 3F **3** (3D **28**)
West Bank YO24: York 4G **27**
Westbourne Gdns. YO8: Sel 3D **58**
Westbourne Gro. YO8: Sel 3D **58**
Westbourne Rd. YO8: Sel 3D **58**
Westbourne Ter. YO8: Sel 3D **58**
West Ct. YO19: Ric 3A **56**
West End YO32: Stre 3H **5**
West End Cl. YO32: Stre 3A **6**
Westerdale Ct. YO30: York 1A **28**
Western Ter. YO32: Hax 1C **10**
West Esplanade
YO1: York 3C **2** (3B **28**)
WEST FIELD 5D **26**
WESTFIELD 4D **58**
Westfield YO8: Sel 3C **58**
Westfield Av. YO8: Sel 3C **58**
Westfield Cl. YO26: Up P 4A **16**
YO32: Wigg 2C **10**
Westfield Ct. YO23: Cop 1C **44**
Westfield Cres. YO26: Tad 3D **54**
Westfield Dr. YO10: York 1D **38**
Westfield Gro. YO32: Wigg 2B **10**
Westfield La. YO26: Up P 3H **15**
YO32: Wigg 2B **10**
Westfield Pl. YO24: York 6C **26**
YO32: Wigg 2C **10**
Westfield Rd. YO8: Sel 3C **58**
YO32: Wigg 2C **10**
Westfield Sq. YO26: Tad 3D **54**
Westfield Ter. YO26: Tad 2D **54**
Westgate YO26: Tad 3D **54**
Westgate Apartments
YO26: York 3B **2** (3B **28**)
Westholme Dr. YO30: York 4G **17**
WEST HUNTINGTON 1C **18**
Westlands Gro. YO31: York 6F **19**
Westminster Pl. YO26: Neth P 4D **16**
Westminster Rd. YO30: York 1A **28**
W. Moor Flats YO19: Ful 3E **39**
W. Moor La. YO10: H'tn 1H **39**
Westmorland Ho. YO24: York 5A **2**
West Mt. YO26: Tad 4D **54**
West Nooks YO32: Hax 2F **11**
West Pk. YO8: Sel 3B **58**
Westpit La. YO32: Stre 4H **5**
West Snickett YO32: Stre 5A **6**
West Thorpe YO24: York 1F **37**
West Vw. YO8: Sel 1H **59**
Westview Cl. YO26: York 6D **16**
West Vw. Mt. YO8: B'by 3F **57**
West Wood La. YO23: Ask B 2G **35**
Westwood M. YO19: Dun 1A **32**
Westwood Ter. YO23: York 6B **28**
Wetherby Rd. YO23: Ruff 3D **24**
YO26: Tad 2C **54**
YO26: York 4C **26**
WHARFE BANK 3E **55**
Wharfe Bank Ter. YO26: Tad 2E **55**
Wharfedale Cres. YO26: Tad 2D **54**
Wharfe Dr. YO24: York 1F **37**
Wharnscliffe Dr. YO30: York 3H **17**
Wharton Av. YO30: York 6B **18**
Wharton Cl. YO41: Stam B 4H **23**
Wharton Rd. YO41: Stam B 4H **23**
Wheatcroft YO32: Stre 5H **5**
Wheatfield La. YO32: Hax 3C **10**
Wheatfields Wlk. YO19: Ric 2B **56**
Wheatlands Gro. YO26: York 1E **27**
Wheatley Dr. YO32: Hax 3C **10**
Wheeldale Dr. YO32: York 3B **20**
Wheelhouse, The YO30: Ske 6D **8**
Wheelwright Cl. YO23: Cop 6D **36**
YO41: Sutt D 1H **51**
WHELDRAKE 5C **50**
Wheldrake La. YO19: Crock H 1H **47**
YO19: Esc 3H **53**
YO19: Whel 6G **49**
YO41: Elv 4D **42**
Whenby Gro. YO31: York 4F **19**
Whernside Av. YO31: York 2G **29**
Whin Cl. YO24: York 2H **37**
YO32: Stre 5A **6**
Whin Gth. YO24: York 3H **37**
Whin Rd. YO24: York 2H **37**
Whip Ma Whop Ma Ga.
YO1: York *3F 3*
(off St Saviourgate)
Whistler Cl. YO23: Cop 6E **37**
Whitby Av. YO31: York 6G **19**
Whitby Dr. YO31: York 6G **19**
Whitecross Gdns. YO31: York 6D **18**
White Cross Rd. YO31: York 6D **18**
White Horse Cl. YO32: Hunt 6F **11**
Whitehouse Ct. *YO30: York* *1B 28*
(off St Olave's Rd.)
White Ho. Dale YO24: York 5H **27**
White Ho. Dr. YO24: York 5H **27**
White Ho. Gdns. YO24: York 5H **27**
White Ho. Gro. YO41: Elv 5F **43**
White Ho. Ri. YO24: York 5H **27**
Whitelands YO32: Ear 3F **11**
Whitelands Cotts.
YO32: Hax 1E **11**
White Lodge YO8: Sel 3C **58**
Whitemoor La. YO8: B'by 2H **57**
White Rose Av. YO32: New E 2D **18**
White Rose Cl. YO26: Neth P 4E **17**
Whiterose Dr. YO41: Stam B 5H **23**
White Rose Gro.
YO32: New E 2D **18**

Printed and bound in the United Kingdom by Gemini Press Ltd., Shoreham-by-Sea, West Sussex
Printed on materials from a sustainable source